HOW TO DESIGN & REMODEL
CHILDREN'S ROOMS

*Created and designed by
the editorial staff of
ORTHO BOOKS*

Project Editor
Christine Dunham

Writers
Anne Levine, Ph.D.
Don Kaplan
Craig A. Bergquist

Illustrator
Gene Takeshita

Photographer
Joyce OudkerkPool

Ortho Books

Publisher
Robert B. Loperena

Editorial Director
Christine Robertson

Production Director
Ernie S. Tasaki

Managing Editors
Robert J. Beckstrom
Michael D. Smith
Sally W. Smith

System Manager
Linda M. Bouchard

Editorial Assistants
Joni Christiansen
Sally J. French

Address all inquiries to
Ortho Books
PO Box 5047
San Ramon, CA 94583

3 4 5 6 7 8 9 10 11
93 94 95 96 97

ISBN 0-89721-143-X
Library of Congress Catalog Card
Number 87-72100

THE SOLARIS GROUP
6001 Bollinger Canyon Road
San Ramon, CA 94583

Acknowledgments

Consultants
Eleanor Criswell, Ph.D.
Louis Kern
Anne Levine, Ph.D.

Copy Chief
Melinda Levine

Copyeditors
Toni Murray
Kate Rider

Proofreader
Andrea Y. Connolly

Production by
Lezlly Freier

Separations by
Color Tech Corporation

Lithographed in USA by
Webcrafters, Inc.

Project Construction

Projects built by
Functional Art, San Francisco, Calif., pages 52, 58–94
Henry Schiff Furniture Mfg. San Pablo, Calif., page 54 (design and construction)

Projects painted by
Haqq Antholzner
Ruth Farrall

Photography

Styling and location scouting
Carol Hacker

Photographic set design
Christine Dunham

Props
Such A Business
Mary Edwards Collection

Additional photographs
Stephen Marley, page 20, 36 (top)
Keith Bradley, page 46 (top)
Doug Manchee, page 46 (bottom)

For a list of Designers and Architects and additional credits, see page 96.

Front cover: Transform an ordinary room into a delightful child's room with effective use of color. See page 10 for more features of this room.

Page 1. A colorful, open wall unit becomes a special showplace.

Page 3. Easel, page 76; Trundle Bed, page 92; Message and Grooming Center, page 86.

Back cover: Clockwise from top left: Toddler's Table and Chairs, page 60; Toddler's Storage Cart, page 58; Storage Center, page 79 and Easel, page 76; Adjustable Study Desk, page 90.

CREATING AN ENVIRONMENT

W**hen designing a child's room, one of the first issues to address is the needs of the child.**

The best way to find out what children consider most important is to talk with them. Ask them how they feel about their rooms, and watch the type of play they engage in most often. From this appraisal will spring many design ideas. Consider the following six basic needs as you talk with and observe your child.

Territory: This Is My Room

Having personal turf is as fundamental as being part of a family. It is a place where the child calls the shots and decides what happens. The child's room signifies a freedom of choice. Personal space is so important that, when not allocated a private room or area, children will often create their own domain by rearranging the furniture or drawing imaginary lines that separate territories. Or they might claim some neutral space in the home, such as a hall closet. The attachment children feel to their personal space is expressed not only by their pleasure in having it, but also in their displeasure with having it taken away or compromised by the addition of a new sibling.

Physical boundaries. When children share a room, they need to know that some part of the room is theirs alone, out of bounds to the rest of the world. It is difficult to set up particular times for ownership of shared property, so physical boundaries are a practical way to establish territory. Space can be demarcated by physical structures, such as room dividers or furniture. A room can be divided equitably by careful placement of screens, sliding doors, curtains, blinds, bookcases, and storage units. These structures can be

Above: *Creative use of a small space turned a light well into an intimate play area. Although the room is small, the skylight and large window contribute to the open, cheerful ambience.*
Left: *Having a little niche where adults cannot fit or cannot enter except by invitation is very satisfying for a child.*

either permanent or temporary, with or without openings for passageways. They should be designed to provide maximum flexibility so that individual spaces can be opened up and shared or closed down at will.

Color. Colors offer another way to zone a room. The use of different colors on the walls, floors, or furniture can signify that one child owns the green side of the room, or all the green furniture, or the drawers with green fronts; another child occupies the yellow zone.

Furniture. Children can have personal space in a shared room. As one woman in the survey remarked, "My bed was my own private place. I could read, study, play, or make a mess there. It felt warm and secure." Drawers or shelves can also be assigned to children separately. One man who shared a room with other family members recalls, "I liked my cedar chest where I could lock up all my toys so my brothers couldn't get them." Closets are often favorite spaces for hiding and playing.

Privacy: Do Not Enter

Part of the reason personal territory is so important to children is that it gives them privacy, the privilege of being alone and unbothered. Many of their waking hours are spent conforming to other people's rules: "Clean up your room. Eat your vegetables. Do your homework. Turn off the television. Go to bed." When children have privacy, they have the opportunity to tune it all out: "Go away world and leave me alone!"

Children need to be themselves, to let down their guards, to view the world from their unique perspectives for a while. They need a time and place to do as they please and to explore their own feelings and thoughts without the expectations or observations of others. When they become old enough to want privacy, it is very important that they are given the means to shut out the world—

Above: Being partially obscured from view by a palm tree instills a sense of privacy for the chalkboard user.
Right: Areas designed for privacy can be built into a room. This cubbyhole was created as part of the built-in bed.

whether it means closing a bedroom door or hiding in a closet. However, take care when considering door locks. Young children can lock doors by mistake and may be unable to unlock them. Also, in the event of fire, no one should have to run around looking for a key to get a child out of the house. Better solutions are to use "Do Not Disturb" signs or to set up rules requiring visitors to knock before entering a room with a closed door.

When children are young, they don't need or want much private time—they want to be near their parents. One young girl lamented, "I don't like being so far away from the other rooms." When they are older, however, the same children often want to be as far away from the family as possible to relax, pursue their interests, or do their homework. "My room was upstairs, away from the family and hullabaloo," commented one man. Another reflected, "My room was down the hall from my parents. I could have phone conversations without being heard."

Whether the child's room is near or far, there are ways to accord privacy. The solution may be as simple as a "Do Not Disturb" sign on the door, or it may require elaborate room dividers and soundproofing.

Basically, there are three aspects of privacy to consider: sight, sound, and space. For some children, just being out of view is what they're really after; for others it may be absolute quiet or just enough room to stretch out unbothered. After talking with your children, determine what is really important to them and plan accordingly.

Identity: Here I Am

Having a chunk of personal space is important for children, but if it is to be truly their own, they need to be able to express their own tastes, interests, and preferences. Throughout the rest of the house they are sur-

rounded by the values and mementos of their parents and other adults. These surroundings are important because they contribute to a sense of family continuity. On the other hand children's rooms are the one place they can personalize with belongings unique to them. For example, photographs of the child with other family members are often viewed as a statement of self-worth within the family structure.

Objects. Children can express their identity simply by having favorite objects in their rooms. Both objects and interests vary from one child to another and from one age to another. An eleven-year-old boy liked to watch his fish; his thirteen-year-old

Children should be encouraged to express their identities. This horsewoman has a place to hang her hat, show off her ribbons, and display a collection of china horses.

Fun and Functional Room Features and Accessories

Bunk beds for over-
night guests, climbing,
and active play

Roller shades to
control light

Colorful, washable
wallcoverings

Full-length mirror
for playacting and
general grooming

Open, stackable
storage bins for
easy access
by youngsters

Closet without doors
for easy use
by young children

Hardwood floor with
area rug for hard and
soft play surfaces

Humorous and practical
child-sized table and stools

Bright, primary colors
for room accents

sister preferred to draw pictures. A six-year-old boy mentioned "my big bear, my lamp bear, my pirate ship, my castle" as his favorite things. One woman in the survey remembered that her room "had two windows side by side and a window box in which I had azaleas and buried my turtles, canaries, and parakeets." Children's rooms should be like sponges that absorb whatever ideas or activities come in them.

Storage. Children like being able to determine how neat or messy their rooms are. Children take great pleasure in their shelves, baskets, closets, cabinets, and desk drawers. In these spaces they can store, find, and display their favorite things. "I like how all my toys are lined up on my bookshelves," commented one six-year-old boy. A different approach was expressed by a man who remembered: "I could keep my room messy.

I could take apart mechanical things and keep the parts in my room." And then there are those caught between clutter and sentiment: "I don't like how cluttered everything is, but I don't want to get rid of anything. I can't bear to do it." That is a dilemma that could be solved by a better storage system.

If parents are unhappy with the messy state of a room, they should ensure that their child has accessible storage space. Slide-out baskets, open shelves, hooks, closet compartments, storage cubes on casters, large bulletin boards, and hanging fabrics with lots of pockets all invite a child to clean up. If it's easy to put things away, children are more likely to do so. Open storage space and easily accessible storage compartments have been shown to work best.

Self-expression. Children express their identities best when they are

encouraged to take an active role in planning their rooms. Of the children and adults interviewed, those most satisfied with their rooms had control of the design process. A fourteen-year-old girl remarked, "There's nothing I don't like about my room because I designed it myself." A seventeen-year-old boy reported that "Everything in my room are things that I've approved of and that reflect my personality and are familiar." One woman remembered, "I loved decorating my room. Painting it and selecting the bedspread gave me a feeling of independence."

Color is one of the most significant aspects of children's rooms and a satisfying means of self-expression. It is easy to apply and simple to change. It makes a room feel warm or cool, dynamic or quiet, large or small, nondescript or personal. The whole tone and mood of a room can be set

Above: *This dresser was designed with handholds and footholds so children can climb it. Here, a small child uses the wall space above the dresser to hang her artwork.*
Right: *Additional shelving above the desk helps keep the work surface uncluttered.*
Opposite: *During planning stages consider features and accessories such as those shown in this photograph.*

by the color. A thirteen-year-old girl complained, "I've had my room since I was five, and everything's pink. Now it gets kind of boring." Children select colors that make them feel good, uplift their spirits, and provide a sense of harmony.

Security:
I Feel Good Here

Everyone needs a place to feel safe and secure, warm and comfortable—a time and a place to reflect on problems, resolve anger and frustration, or just turn down the surrounding sights and sounds.

There are many different design elements that contribute to a peaceful room. Wall and floor insulation can help make a room quiet enough for children to hear "the summer sounds of birds and crickets" or "the foghorns in the morning." A rope swing or rocking chair can relax their bodies. Staring at the wallcovering or the view outside the window can provide rhythmic patterns conducive to daydreaming or emptying their minds. Windows do more than just offer a resting place for gazing eyes: They let in the light and the warmth of the sun. Color, fabrics, and upholstered furniture also lend a quiet ambience to a room or part of a room.

The size of a room also contributes to the feeling of security. Although a large room may make a child feel important, a small room may be preferred. One thirteen-year-old boy likes his room because "it's small and cozy and warm." However, if a room is large, the design can incorporate nooks and crannies in which to snuggle without compromising the light, airy feeling that a large room can impart.

It's important to include a space for you, the parent, to sit when you are with your children in their rooms. The fact that you are comfortable when enjoying the time spent with a child enhances your positive feelings and the sense of security that makes the room a friendly place.

Above: Cozy, partially enclosed spaces make a child feel secure.
Right: For a baby, nothing is quite so secure as snuggling in mother's lap.
Opposite: The advantages of a mattress on the floor are threefold: It is a safe distance off the floor; it offers a soft space on which to sit quietly and play; and it is terrific for bouncing, rolling, and tumbling on.

Stimulation: Let's Play

In contrast to the time for quiet and repose, children also need to express their noisy and exuberant side. One man liked his childhood room because "there was plenty of space and we could have good pillow fights." Young children tend to prefer thrilling physical activity that tests their strength and dexterity; they enjoy climbing up and down structures, sliding down poles, jumping on beds, squeezing through small spaces, hanging precariously, throwing missiles, rolling down foam slabs, and hiding in secret niches. They also like to challenge their minds and hands, pouring themselves into creative and imaginative projects, such as building geometric structures, completing puzzles, performing in a puppet theater, experimenting with magnets, pasting together collages, and playing musical instruments.

Floor space is one of the most important ingredients required to satisfy the needs for physical and mental stimulation. One sports fan reminisced, "I liked my green carpet because I could pretend it was a baseball field." Ideally, a child's room should have some hard and some soft floor space. The hard surface makes it easier to play with objects such as rolling toys, stacking blocks, and small standing figures. The soft surface is more comfortable for tumbling, rolling, and playing large board games.

Another significant design feature is a good work space with storage capacity. As one youngster commented: "I like my desk. Everything I do gets done there. It's big and can store things."

Fun and Functional Room Features and Accessories

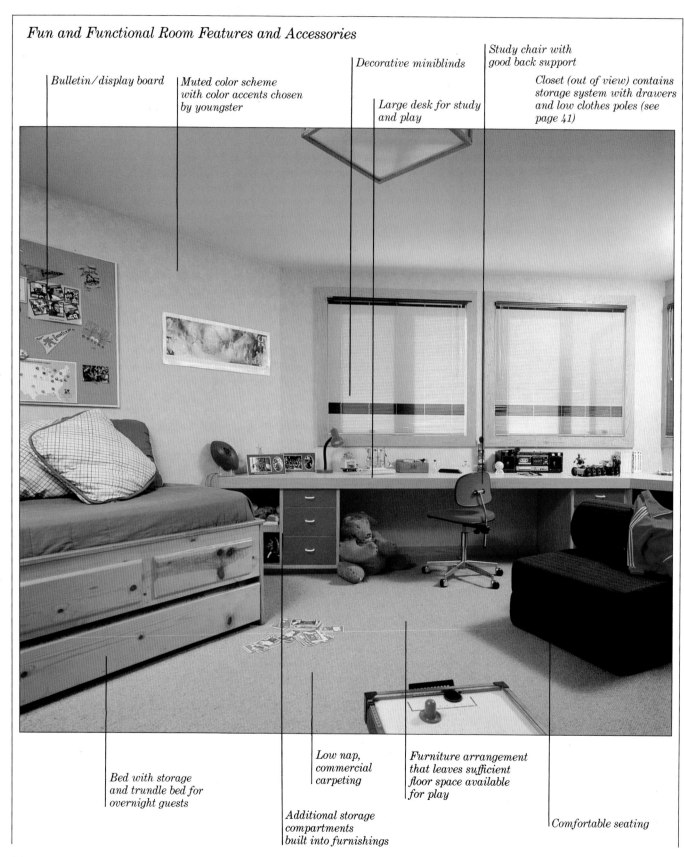

Bulletin/display board

Muted color scheme with color accents chosen by youngster

Decorative miniblinds

Large desk for study and play

Study chair with good back support

Closet (out of view) contains storage system with drawers and low clothes poles (see page 41)

Bed with storage and trundle bed for overnight guests

Additional storage compartments built into furnishings

Low nap, commercial carpeting

Furniture arrangement that leaves sufficient floor space available for play

Comfortable seating

Above: *Displays of favorite collectibles, such as these playbills, will spark conversation during a friend's visit. Soft cushions and rugs on the floor make comfortable seating.*
Opposite: *Once children start school, a study area needs to be defined along with the other activity areas in a room. This room has a large study desk as a built-in feature.*

Sociability: Please Come In

Children don't always want to "do their thing" alone. Often they prefer to share their interests and activities with a family member or a friend. Young friends are usually quite happy playing or sitting on the floor, but don't forget to allow for making adults comfortable, too. That usually means adequate adult-sized seating, whether it be an armchair, bed, bench, or platform. Bending over and sitting on the floor are uninviting alternatives for some parents, who are not comfortable doing so.

It is important for children to have their parents come to their turf, where the children have control and are surrounded by representations of their identities. Children need to be able to show off their prowess, their collections, and their accomplishments, which stand out more readily in their own rooms than anywhere else in the house.

Sharing a room with a family member presents advantages and disadvantages. It can be a wonderful experience. One woman remembered, "I shared a room with my sister. I loved whispering secrets to her at night when we were in our beds and it was dark and quiet." But, sharing a room can also be infuriating. One respondent bemoaned, "When I shared a room with my brother, it was always messy and I got blamed for it." Another commented, "I shared my room with my two brothers and we were all squashed together." If a room is well planned, sharing won't be a test of wills; it can foster closeness between siblings as well as serve as valuable experience for learning the art of compromise and negotiation. Children with very different personalities may never see eye to eye, but they can get along.

Children also like to invite their friends over for the afternoon or night. Inviting friends over builds a special closeness and trust in the relationship. One youngster fondly recalls, "I slept high up on the bunk bed. My friends slept underneath." Ideally, a room should be designed to allow for "sleepover" visitors. Bunk beds, trundle beds, sofa beds, and futons provide sleeping space for guests. If children share a room, finding extra sleeping space becomes more complicated but not impossible—there are always sleeping bags and the floor.

record player
TV

cage

pool

diving
bord

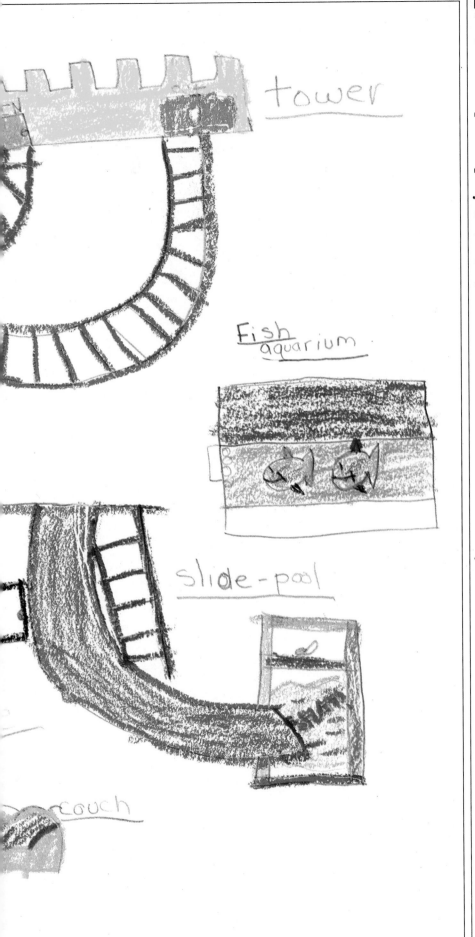

tower

Fish aquarium

slide-pool

couch

PLANNING

Designing a child's room can be an enjoyable project for both parents and children. Whether the theme you choose is a fairy-tale scene, a futuristic landscape, or a traditional setting, you want the room to be a comfortable, stimulating, and safe environment that will contribute to the quality of your child's life.

Although there's no one way to do it right, a well-planned room will help your child develop his or her abilities and strengths and provide opportunities for learning at every stage of development.

The decor does not need to be elaborate to capture a child's imagination. Simple themes can work well, especially if children participate in the design process and the room allows for their special interests.

Emi, age 7
Pacific Grove, California

DESIGNING TOGETHER

Y ou might have a dozen great ideas for transforming the room into a scene from the Wizard of Oz, but your child may have no desire whatsoever to follow the yellow brick road you had planned to paint on the floor.

Your child's interests (within reason) should be foremost, because ultimately he or she is the one who will live in the room. The best way to design a room that pleases both of you is to talk about it. Older children can help plan their rooms by discussing what they like. Try some of the following questions: Would you prefer plain or patterned walls? Do you like curtains or blinds? What colors do you like most and least? If you could change anything about your room, what would it be?

A discussion of habits, priorities, when and how the room is used, and current as well as past interests will affect the way you plan the room. You might also want to talk with your child about how much everything will cost. This discussion will help your youngster develop a sense of responsibility for the room and practice consumer skills while working towards a goal.

Use your child's current interests and hobbies as a starting point for a design. For example, if he or she enjoys reading or is an avid collector, you'll want to plan plenty of shelves for books and displays. If there is an interest in science or plants, try setting up space under the windows for science experiments, or a miniature greenhouse. You might want to develop the design around a single theme, such as a favorite storybook character. Just keep in mind that interests may change quickly, and satisfaction in the theme may be

short-lived. A compromise would be to incorporate the theme into furnishings and decorations that can easily be replaced, such as posters, bed sheets, and wall graphics.

Even though very young children might not be able to describe clearly how they would like their room to look, you can discover their interests by looking at their artwork and watching them play. What do they spend most of their time doing? Do certain colors dominate their artwork? Do they play with one type of toy more often than others? What are their favorite records or picture books? Design ideas could arise from any of these sources and serve as a motif for the room.

No matter what theme is chosen, don't involve the whole room with one concept so that everything is set up. It will hamper your child's imagination. Leave some of the design ambiguous so that your child has a space in which to use his or her creativity.

Talking with your child about the design is the best way to make sure a room meets both the child's and the family's needs. The use of a variety of color and designing aids, such as a color wheel and furniture diagrams, makes the decision-making process much easier.

ASSESSING THE ROOM

Whatever the shape of the room, you can make it safe and comfortable for children. By examining the physical structure, you will discover limitations as well as elements that will stimulate your imagination for decorative schemes.

Before you start, ask yourself a few general questions.

Will children be sharing the room? If so, what are their ages, and personal needs? (See pages 24–25 about dividing a room.)

What kinds of activities does your child usually like to do in the room? (See pages 26–27 for plan drawings.)

What furniture do you have that you would like to use? (See pages 46–47 about furniture.)

How much time do you have to spend on this project? Do you have space and tools to create unique or built-in furniture? (See pages 49–94 for project ideas.)

How much money do you want to spend? (See pages 22–23 about pre-planning.)

Your answers to these questions and those on the accompanying checklist will help you plan a workable design that will meet the needs of your child and the entire family.

Checklist for Room Evaluation

Size and Shape

How large is the room? What feeling do you get from it? Is it warm and inviting or austere? Does it have a pleasing or awkward shape? Is it large enough to incorporate a play area or changing room?

A large room for a small child can be scary, and the space may have to be broken up by dividers or modular units to make it warm and manageable. Conversely, you can make a small, cramped room appear larger and brighter by using color, light, and furniture placement.

Light and Ventilation

Is the room airy and well ventilated? Do the windows allow much light? Where does the light fall?

It is important to have plenty of fresh air in the room. In a poorly ventilated room, you might be able to add a window or a ceiling fan to increase air circulation. The direction the room faces, the amount of natural light it receives, and where the light falls affect the window treatment and the placement of artificial lighting.

Architectural Features

Does the room have any built-in features (such as a radiator or sloped ceiling) that must be incorporated into your design? What kind of storage space can the closet provide? Are cupboard shelves deep enough to store clothing and large objects, or are they shallow (in which case they may be useful for displaying collections)?

Unless you own your home and can afford renovations, you will probably have to live with existing architectural features. Try to accentuate the best features of the room by using colors or decorations that will make them stand out; disguise existing faults by using colors that blend into the background, or camouflage them with movable screens.

Condition

Are there any structural problems that need to be repaired? What is the condition of the walls and window frames? Do the walls need soundproofing? What is the floor like? If the floor is wood, does it need to be sanded? Do any floorboards need to be replaced? Are there holes in the skirting boards that need to be filled?

The condition of the walls and whether they are rough or smooth will help you decide whether to use paint or wallcovering. Be sure to check the walls and ceiling for dampness. If the room is drafty or if noise is a problem, the floor or walls may need to be insulated. If it isn't practical to insulate the walls in your child's room, it might be possible to insulate the adjoining room.

Heating

Is heating adequate? Is a radiator or electrical heating unit exposed? Does it become too hot to touch?

The temperature of the room should be even—65° to 70° F is ideal under normal conditions. Do not leave heating units exposed; cover them with screens or guards that are appropriate for small children. If you are adding an additional heat source, make sure it is UL tested and permanently affixed. Portable heaters are not recommended for use in children's rooms.

Electrical Outlets

Are there enough outlets for intended uses?

Although one or two outlets may be fine for an infant's room, they will probably be insufficient when your child begins to read and use electronic equipment and games. Extension cords and long, trailing wires are a hazard and should not be used in children's rooms. The need for more outlets indicates the need for proper rewiring.

Adequate heating in the room is important for a child of any age, but it is especially important for a newborn. Take care of heating concerns before the baby arrives.

Heating

Newborns lose body heat much faster than do adults, and they cannot move around or shiver efficiently to generate heat. Conversely, if the room is too warm, the baby will breath rapidly and physiological systems can be thrown out of balance, so keeping a consistent room temperature day and night is important. The newborn needs as many calories as possible for growth and development; caloric energy should not be wasted in trying to keep warm or cool down.

Before the baby comes home, install a wall thermometer in the room and experiment with your heating system until a consistent temperature between 65° and 70° F can be maintained. A temperature of 70° F is ideal for most of the newborn's activities; raise the temperature to 80° F for bathing.

If you determine that your child's room is subject to uneven heating because of construction or location in the house, adding a single-room heat source may be wise. Consider installing adequate wall- or floor-mounted heaters that have been tested with child safety in mind. Place them near the areas of greatest heat loss, such as under windows, to facilitate even heating.

Correct unnecessary heat loss from windows, doors, and chimneys with weather stripping and similar products that are designed for this purpose. (Remember, you don't want to completely seal out fresh air, so follow manufacturer's suggestions.)

If the room is subject to floor drafts, the use of a decorative stuffed "draft stopper" would be most welcome for your toddler, who will spend a great deal of time on the floor. If you must keep the door closed to reduce drafts, consider installing a Dutch door. The lower half can remain closed with the draft stopper in place, while the top is open to allow fresh air and visibility.

Electrical Systems

After you have assessed the room, it's time to check the electrical system once again to see if it can accommodate all that you and your child have in mind for the future. Remember, do not use extension cords or long, trailing cords for lights and accessories. Permanently wire as many fixtures as possible, and be sure to install electrical outlets close to activity areas that will require them.

For a newborn or toddler, general ceiling light with a dimmer switch is all that is really necessary. In addition, a childproof night-light is a convenience because it keeps low light in the room at all hours of the night. Some night-lights provide enough light for midnight feedings and diaper changes.

Preschoolers and school-age children need task-oriented lighting at the site of activity, such as a lamp for reading in bed, building models on the worktable, and playing games on the floor.

In general, consider the location of wall- and ceiling-mounted lights, and then install permanent wiring—leaving the choice of fixture subservient to the task it will be lighting. Easy-to-install surface-mounted wiring can be used as a decorative element in a child's room if it is coordinated as part of the room design. For installation and wiring techniques, see Ortho's *Basic Wiring Techniques*.

Even if all you need now is an overhead light, plan for future needs such as a computer and reading lamps.

Safety First

As you plan your design, keep safety foremost in your mind. Injuries happen because of poor planning. When children become absorbed in their activities they don't think about safety; it is up to you to plan ahead for them. The safety precautions you must take depend on a child's stage of development, which is not necessarily related to the age of the child. Remember, if there is some way to get into, out of, under, or on top of something, there's a child who can figure out how to do it!

Cribs

Check the construction on an infant's crib. Make sure that slats are not more than 2⅜ inches apart so that small heads can't get stuck between them. Use childproof latches so that drop sides can't be released by the infant or other young siblings. The mattress should be firm, and there should be no dangerous gaps between the mattress and the sides of the crib. (If you can insert two fingers between the mattress and the crib side, the mattress is too small.) If bumper pads are used, make sure there are at least six straps to provide a secure fit. Also, don't use thin plastic to protect crib mattresses from wetness; the plastic can cause suffocation.

Look for cribs with the highest side rails—a minimum of 22 inches is recommended from the top of the railing to the mattress set at its lowest level. As soon as more than one quarter of the child's height extends beyond the top rail, move the child to a low bed with guardrails.

Avoid cribs with corner treatments that could snag clothing. Corner posts should not extend more than ⅝ inch above the end panel.

As soon as children are old enough to pull themselves up on hands and knees, remove any crib gyms that stretch across the crib.

Never hang decorations or toys with long strings or ribbons in the crib.

Don't leave large toys in the crib; older babies may use them as steps to climb out of the crib.

Don't leave the crib gate down or unlocked whenever the infant is left in the crib.

A damaged or splintered railing can be dangerous for a teething child who may chew on it. Repair or replace damaged parts.

Other Features

□ If you are adding outlets to a room, they should be high on the wall, out of the reach of toddlers. Existing outlets should be covered with safety covers so that children can't put fingers or objects into them. Keep freestanding lights and appliances out of the way and avoid using extension cords. Night-lights are comforting as well as practical.
□ Radiators and electric heaters should always be shielded so that toddlers can't touch or fall on them.
□ Windows, even at ground level, are a hazard and should have childproof locks (various types are available for different windows). In low windows, put up a temporary screen or a device with vertical bars closely spaced so small heads can't get stuck between them. The device should be made of nontoxic material and be removable in the event of fire. Don't position chairs or other climbable furniture under windows. Avoid long curtains that toddlers could pull down or trip over. Use flame-resistant or flame-retardant textiles and linings in the child's room and throughout the house.
□ Toddlers often chew on furniture, so be certain that paints and finishes are nontoxic and lead free. Most paints in the United States are now lead free, but there are many that still contain toxic pigments or other toxins, so look for the words *nontoxic*, *lead free*, and *child safe*.

□ Check for flaws and torn areas that expose stuffing in upholstery, mattresses, toys, or other items that infants might teeth on.
□ Do not decorate a small child's room with ornaments that can be swallowed.
□ Toy chests can be especially dangerous for children under the age of two. A toy chest should not have a latch or lock that could trap a child inside. Be certain that the chest is ventilated in such a way that the holes won't be blocked if the chest is placed against a wall. If the toy chest has a lid, it should be lightweight and attached with hinges that will keep it open in any position so that it can't fall unexpectedly.
□ Don't put young children (usually under five) in the upper bunk. Make sure the ladder to the upper bunk is secure.
□ Shelves should be fastened securely to the wall since children may try to climb them. Keep a step stool handy.
□ Make sure all furniture is stable and cannot be knocked over. Fasten tall bureaus, chests, and bookcases directly to the wall. Eliminate or avoid buying furniture with sharp points or corners. Make sure wooden chairs are splinter-free.
□ Any fixtures hung from the ceiling should be fastened securely to overhead joists or rafters.
□ Use nonslip polish on wood or tiled floors. Don't leave lumpy rugs with curled edges in a child's room since they are easily tripped over.
□ Install smoke detectors.
□ The United States Consumer Product Safety Commission produces a wealth of information about product safety as well as tips on household safety. For more information, write to: U.S. Consumer Product Safety Commission, Washington, D.C. 20207. To report a problem or a product you feel is unsafe, call 800-638-2772.

PLANNING AHEAD

Children's rooms have to be planned differently than rooms for adults because children's needs and interests change at different stages of development. Yet upgrading your child's room doesn't have to be an expensive venture.

Keep adaptability in mind. With a little planning and imagination, your efforts won't be wasted in a few years when your child grows into his or her next stage. By thinking ahead now, you can plan for your child's changing needs, keep costs down and frustration to a minimum, and make your youngster think you're the greatest.

During the early years children need a sense of security; they also like to spread out on the floor to play. Later, children need spaces to work, display collections, and store books and school materials. A child's room is always a diverse activity center that often has to be shared with a brother or sister. And, of course, there are all those possessions that need to be stored away.

Infant's and Toddler's Needs

Until infants begin to crawl, they need very little in the way of furnishings and space. An infant's room can be furnished simply with storage units, a crib, a changing table, a rocking chair, and a wheeled cart for storing and moving toiletries and diapers to where you need them.

Colorful wall treatments and mobiles for the crib are inexpensive, effective stimulation for an infant. The top of a chest of drawers makes a handy surface for changing the baby, and the chest will last for many years beyond the diaper stage. Adult-sized comfortable seating is essential for feeding the newborn and later, when you read to your toddler. Carpeting is warm and cozy but impractical for young children, especially if they have allergies. Consider a more durable flooring, such as wood or vinyl, that will last through the preschool years. You may want to add a small area rug for comfort.

Toddlers (ages one to three) need a stimulating environment that still provides a sense of security and stability. Since they are beginning to explore their environment for themselves, design elements and objects should be available at their level. Bright, warm

---

If you look at a room with long-term goals in mind, you'll find many ways to renew the space without a great deal of expense or effort. Follow the stages of the room at right. With only a few furniture changes and a little paint, the room accommodates the various needs of a growing child. Note how the dressers are used for a changing table in Phase I; a dresser in Phase II; and a desk in Phase III. The open storage on the floor is added to in Phase II, and then moved to the wall in Phase III. It is helpful to start with a list of items that you feel are essential and a separate list of those that are desirable to you.

Phase I: Newborn to three year olds

closet

Essential: *Adult-sized rocker; changing table and storage; crib; safety devices (such as window guards and heat screens).*
Desirable: *Colorful mobile; decorative wallcoverings; cradle for newborn; movable storage cart; area rug.*

colors and decorations along the lower half of furniture and walls are at eye level for the toddler. Open storage and low toy carts allow access to playthings and cuddlies.

Since the early exploration stage can be a dangerous time, take precautions. Install window safety bars that can easily be removed in case of fire, place covers over electrical outlets, and provide a bed with a safety rail to prevent accidents. (For more information on safety, see Safety First on page 21.)

Preschooler's Needs

Floor space is critical for both toddlers and preschoolers, who spend a lot of time in their rooms performing a variety of activities. For this age group (ages three to six), you need to divide the room into activity and rest areas, and you may want to change colors to freshen the room. Mounting a chalkboard and paper roll on the lower half of one wall encourages creative expression without jeopardizing the whole room. An easy-to-clean, durable flooring is important at this stage.

Preschoolers have lots of toys, and you can add open units, stacking boxes, plastic cubes or crates, and adjustable shelves for storage as well as to encourage tidiness. During this stage children enjoy what is known as dramatic play, which involves role-playing a variety of characters. Providing space to hang hats and display costumes that are easily reached will add to their play.

School-Age Children's Needs

Although school-age children (ages six to eleven) still need space to play in, work surfaces and a comfortable chair or two become important. The space formerly used for changing diapers can be set up as a work area or dressing table. The diaper and toy cart can now be used to hold a TV and VCR or other electronic equipment. Children at this stage begin collecting all kinds of things. They begin to personalize their identity, and they take a great deal of pride in their accomplishments. Adequate display areas will help meet these needs. Shelves that were used for toys can now be raised or supplemented to display collections, projects, and to store books. Corkboards provide a versatile means of display that can be changed daily. The addition of a rug, new window and wall treatments, and bunk beds or a trundle bed for friends who sleep over also help meet a child's changing needs. You might want to consider adding modular units that can be rearranged in a variety of configurations.

Phase II: Three to six year olds

Phase III: Six to eleven year olds

Essential additions: *More open storage; table and chairs; full-sized bed with guardrail.*
Desirable additions: *Chalkboard and corkboard; costume and hat rack; new color for walls; climbing frame.*

Essential additions: *Study desk; chair with good back support; reading lights; display shelves; new color for walls.*
Desirable additions: *Extra bed for guests; area rug or carpeting; guest seating.*

DIVIDING SPACE

*Y*ou might need room dividers if you are sharing your room with your infant, if two children are sharing one room, if a large space needs to be broken up for privacy and manageability (many children prefer small, cozy spaces that make them feel secure), or to divide a room into separate sleep and activity areas.

Dividers come in a variety of shapes and can be made from a variety of materials. Keep in mind that color and the way furniture is arranged can provide psychological, if not physical, divisions.

If you need to divide a room for siblings to share, investigate the situation before deciding what type of divider to use. The temperaments of children, even though they are in the same family, may vary greatly. Likewise, the need for privacy and territory differs from child to child. Some require only a hint of privacy and possession; others require more. Teaching children to be thoughtful of others' belongings and cooperative about sharing space can go a long way toward keeping conflicts down to a minimum, but it won't necessarily eliminate them—sometimes a permanent, substantial divider is the best solution. Examine your children's behavior, talk to them, and try to assess the range of privacy and territory desired. If one has strong feelings about visual privacy (not being seen), a temporary or partial visual barrier may be all that is needed. If, on the other hand, both have strong feelings about being seen and heard, build a permanent, substantial divider.

It's fairly easy to color code storage, label belongings, and delineate space with color and furniture arrangement. But it can be difficult—if not impossible—to physically divide a room if it is not large enough or if the windows and doors will not allow an acceptable division. In this case it might be worth trading rooms with your children if your room is larger; it may be easier to divide the space and keep the peace. If dividing the room permanently is out of the question, there are many effective compromises that can be arranged: using temporary dividers, arranging private space elsewhere in the house, scheduling time to be in the room alone, and clearly defining personal belongings and study space.

Permanent Dividers
Some ideas for permanent dividers include the following.
□ A row of low storage units or cubes extended across the floor can double as a work surface. A shade or blind that hangs from the ceiling over these units creates additional privacy.
□ A floor-to-ceiling shelving unit with shelves on both sides incorporates horizontal and vertical dividers. The stored items on shelves and in cubicles also help to absorb sound.
□ Two wardrobes placed side to side with the backs facing in opposite directions are an effective room divider. The backs can be decorated with posters, a bulletin board or pegboard, or used for storage like the back of a door (see page 39).
□ A whole wall or half wall can be made from wallboard. Circles, squares, or slits can be cut into the divider for decoration, play space, or ventilation.
□ Painted and shaped plywood cutouts create imaginative barriers.
□ Beds can be placed back to back with a plywood divider, open shelving, or with back-to-back bookcases in between.

This room divider is part of an unusual bunk bed. The top bunk overhangs the lower bed and is part of the permanent room divider. This substantial structure gives visual as well as audio privacy.

Whatever type of divider or barrier you decide on, make sure that light, heat, and air circulation are sufficient in all areas. Designing the divider so you can look through from one area to the other will make the room seem less cramped and aid air circulation. Also, be certain that permanent dividers are securely fixed and won't collapse if climbed on.

Temporary Dividers

If you need a temporary divider or one that can be moved out of the way, a blackboard on casters or accordian-style doors will work well. Curtains attached to metal rails can be drawn for privacy, or loose fabric panels fixed at the ceiling can be easily brushed out of the way. Japanese folding screens of wood and paper divide space attractively. Make your own screens by using fabric and wood stretcher bars, which are available in art supply stores.

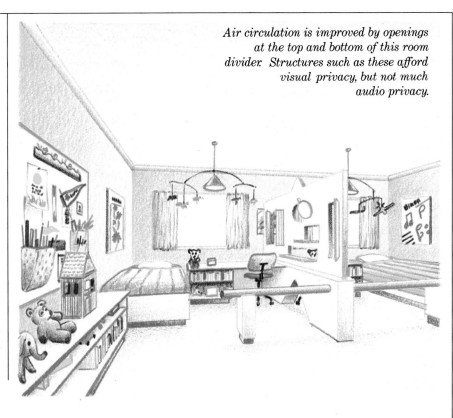

Air circulation is improved by openings at the top and bottom of this room divider. Structures such as these afford visual privacy, but not much audio privacy.

Folding screens make useful temporary dividers. They offer privacy, and it is easy to find or make one that will fit into your room design.

Movable panels in this divider allow the space to be opened up or divided at will.

PLAN DRAWINGS

Working out your ideas for a design on paper can help you visualize what the room will look like. Drawings will also help you work out progressive plans for future changes, such as additional children or more grown-up tastes.

To make a floor plan, you'll need blank paper and tracing paper, a pad of graph paper, a soft-lead pencil, a 25-foot metal tape measure, and a ruler. You might want to use some additional supplies that make drawing the plan easier: an architect's rule (which translates dimensions directly into whatever scale you want to use), a triangle, a compass, and hard-lead pencils for making fine lines.

Gleaning ideas. Interview your child and make a list of activities your child does (or will be doing) in the room. You might divide the list into functions (such as grooming, resting, playing, and working). This list will help you plan the size necessary for each activity area and accompanying furnishings.

Sketching the plan. Do a rough sketch on blank paper. Using your activity list, represent each activity grouping on paper with a circle, and use arrows to show the traffic patterns (pathways) they create. (Doors, closets, and built-ins create natural traffic patterns.) Don't worry about scale, size, or shape at this point; use the sketch, which is called a bubble drawing, to see how spaces relate to one another. Focus on how your child will move through the spaces and how much floor, play, and work

space you need to provide. Experiment with various arrangements, keeping in mind the different activities that will take place and where they should be. Create as many different sketches as possible.

Refining the plan. Convert the rough sketch into a refined plan that takes into account the dimensions of the room. Measure and draw built-in

storage areas, indicating the swing of doors, and heating units. Note the location of outlets, light switches, and light fixtures. Draw this plan freehand (it is only intended as a guide), using the graph paper to keep the proportions accurate. Write the dimensions on the plan as you go along. A convenient scale for most plans is ¼ inch to the foot. You'll find it

Bubble Diagram

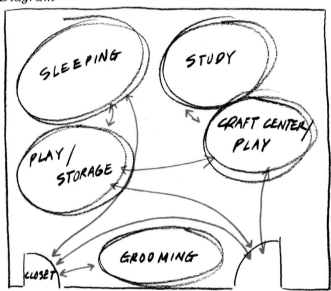

Refining the Plan

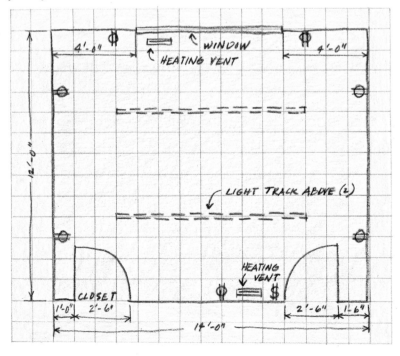

helpful to use paper lined to the scale you are using (that is, each square should be ¼ inch wide) and to note the scale on the plan.

Drawing the final plan. Before you draw the first line, decide how to position the plan so it fits on the paper. Standard practice is to draw the plan with north at the top or on the left side. Start by rendering the overall dimensions of the room, and work your way down to details. Measure the length and width of the room, the distance of doors and windows from the end of a wall and from each other, and the width of door and window moldings.

Draw a line for each wall, leaving the proper amount of space for each door or window. Draw in the windows and doors. Swinging doors should be shown in the open position (draw a quarter circle from the hinges to show the swing; use a semicircle if the door swings both ways). A sepa-

rate elevation plan for storage walls will also be useful. Use the width measurements from your floor plan and add height measurements.

Testing the plan. Finally, clip a piece of tracing paper over the graph paper of the floor plan and draw in the essential furniture. Refine the layout by retracing the sections of the plan you want to keep and adding sections as you try new layouts. Be sure that furniture doesn't block windows, doors, or closets and that there is enough clearance for opening things, making the bed, and pulling out chairs. After you've drawn a plan you're satisfied with, you might want to make a more precise version on another sheet of graph paper.

With your plan in hand, walk through the room with your child and evaluate the design. Is the room comfortable and functional? Have you maximized floor space? Will your child be able to move easily through the room? Are any aspects of the room overwhelming?

Final Plan With Tissue Overlay

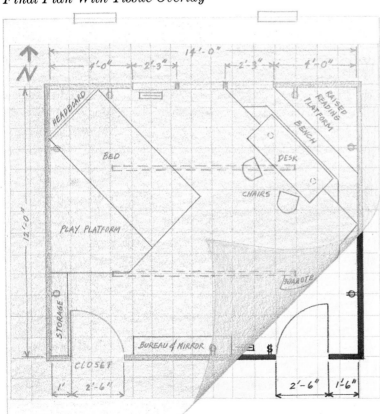

Elevation Drawing

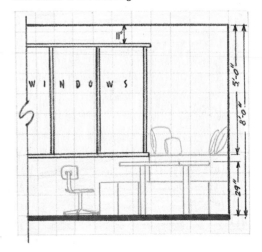

27

Play ar

Fish Tank

PUTTING IT ALL TOGETHER

By helping children plan their living space, parents give them the opportunity to express themselves, to accommodate personality development and social needs, and to feel secure and respected.

Every child has a unique creative sense. It is fun for children, as well as their parents, to explore individual ideas and creations.

The following chapter illustrates ideas for using color, painting floors and walls, covering windows, decorating doors, creating storage, and lighting a room. It also shows how to size furniture for children. Selective use of design elements make rooms for children especially inviting.

Michelle, age 9½
Clearlake, Illinois

USING COLOR

When deciding which colors to use in your child's room, you might want to consider what research has shown concerning the effects of color on children's behavior. Most important, however, you'll want to talk to your child about color preferences.

Small children respond to and are stimulated by color. Primary colors have proven to be the traditional favorites of young children—almost all love bright, bold colors as part of their environment. Psychologists assert that a room with hot colors (such as red and orange) can stimulate a passive child, and a room with cool colors (such as blue, green, and gray) can have a calming influence on an overactive child.

Remember the color wheel you learned about in elementary school? It showed the three primary colors—red, yellow, and blue—and the secondary colors created by combining the primary colors. Complementary colors (those directly opposite each other on the wheel) create contrast and seem more vivid when used next to each other. Analogous colors (those next to each other on the circle) blend and are compatible. Colors in the blue family are cool and calming. Reds, oranges, and browns are rich and warm. Grays and purples are warm, too, but formal. The amount of yellow or blue in a color can change the effect. Blues and greens with a lot of yellow in them can seem warm, and reds or yellows with a great deal of blue can appear cool.

When choosing colors, pay particular attention to the hues, values, and intensities of colors you are selecting. Hue refers to the name of the color, such as yellow or green, and where it appears on the color wheel. Value refers to the lightness or darkness of a color on a scale from white to black. Intensity refers to the brightness or impact of a color.

Color is affected by everything around it. There are no hard and fast rules for successful color combinations. It takes time and experimentation to understand how your color selections will work with each other. The best way to select a range of colors is to place them side by side so that the value and intensity can be directly compared under the same light conditions. You will be able to see if they compete, complement, or cancel each other out. A color wheel or color chips are extremely useful in the absence of the actual products or materials you are considering. Take the color wheel or chips with you as you consider each item to be placed in the room.

You can choose colors that create particular moods or colors that work well in dark or light spaces. For a contrasting scheme, choose one color for the large areas of the room and a second, contrasting color, for furnishings and accessories. (If you use both colors equally, they will fight each

The bright yellow walls add interest and have the advantage of reflecting light in this small room.

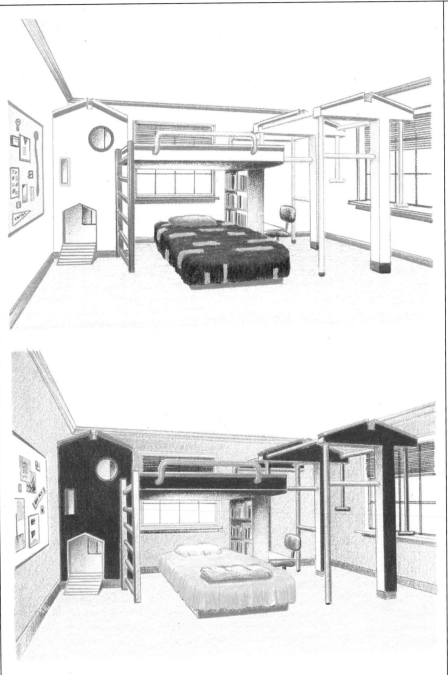

These two rooms look quite different, but their structural components are exactly the same. Not only does the choice of color affect the feel of the room, it affects the perception of the components by emphasizing or de-emphasizing them.

other for attention.) For a harmonizing scheme, choose from one color family for the entire room.

When choosing colors, consider the quality of light in the room. If the room receives cool northern or eastern light, which makes cool colors appear even cooler, you might want to use warm colors to counterbalance the effect. If the room receives warm southern or western light, you might want to cool down the effect by using cool colors where the light falls.

Here are some other points to consider when planning color.

☐ The larger the area you color, the more it will dominate and distract from other elements of the room.

☐ Too many colors can make a room unnecessarily busy.

☐ Use simple furnishings with bold-colored walls, and be careful that vivid colors don't become overwhelming.

☐ In a room with a uniform color, use color highlights and textures in the furniture and accessories.

☐ Use color to divide space and define territories. A play area can be separated from a sleeping area by painting it a different shade or color; two sleeping areas or private play territories can be marked off in a similar way. If two children share a room, you might want to use a different dominant color for each child's area and unify both areas with a common color as part of the design.

☐ Color affects the way we perceive space. Cool, neutral colors can make a small room look larger than it is; therefore, light grays, white, and pastels are good choices for a small room. Strong, warm colors can make a room look smaller, but using them selectively will liven it up. White makes a ceiling appear higher and helps other colors seem more vivid. Strips of color used vertically will emphasize height; horizontal strips will emphasize width and length.

SURFACE TREATMENTS

*N*o matter what your decorating style, you can add individuality and charm to any child's room. The fixed elements, such as floors and walls, can be planned as a cohesive whole or singled out for special focus.

The choice of materials and the way they are applied can have great impact on the appeal of a room. Following are examples of treatments for floors, walls and ceilings, windows, and doors.

Floors

The floor is the most used surface of a young child's room—in fact, children spend most of their time on the floor. They love to lie, sit, crawl, draw, and look at books on it, surrounded by their playthings.

Even after they start school, children continue to spend a great deal of time on the floor, involved in all kinds of activities. Floors need to look good and be able to withstand the various abuses they will be subject to each day. For children of any age, the type of flooring selected should be easy to maintain, comfortable to play on, reasonably warm and free from drafts, nonslip, smooth, and as sound absorbent as possible.

Wood
Wood is easy to maintain, attractive, and a good surface for all kinds of activities, such as wheeling, building, and drawing. When the floor is smooth and free of splinters, it can be stained, waxed, painted, or coated with polyurethane. Keep in mind that wood floors are noisy and that babies

who are just learning to walk and wearing socks or footed pajamas may slip and slide at first.

Vinyl Sheet and Tile
Available in a wide variety of colors, patterns, and prices, vinyl flooring materials are a good choice. They are hard wearing, easy to maintain, and have either a textured or a smooth surface. Cushion-backed vinyls are best for sound insulation and the most comfortable underfoot. They are fairly cool to the touch, but provide for maximum freedom of activity. Vinyl composition is less expensive than solid or cushion-backed vinyl, but it is not as sound absorbant or resilient.

Vinyl-Coated Cork
Cork flooring comes in a limited range of natural cork colors, but its attractive appearance coordinates well with most decors. The vinyl coating results in a smooth surface that allows for easy maintenance. Cork flooring is fairly soft and warm to the touch, and is good for sound insulation. Although it is fairly expensive, surface and sound insulation qualities make it a good choice.

Carpet
Rugs and carpets are warm and cozy, but they are impractical for young children. A thick-pile carpet may be good for crawling on, but it also holds dust that can be unhealthy for an infant to breathe. Even carpet that has been treated to resist stains is not easy to clean. Rugs and carpets limit the activities your child can perform. They are hard to wheel and push toys over and provide a poor surface for balancing blocks, building, drawing, and putting together puzzles. Small rugs, when held in place with nonslip backing, can provide soft ''islands'' on a hard floor.

If you want to buy a carpet for an infant's or preschooler's room, consider a low-pile, medium-toned carpet, which will show less dirt than dark or light colors. For easy care and a better play surface, you might also

consider using a low-pile synthetic industrial carpet. Ideally, use carpeting for the sleeping area and another flooring material for the play area.

If a good-quality carpet has already been laid, you can protect it by covering activity areas with a sheet of vinyl or a rubber mat. You might also use a standard office chair mat that allows chairs to roll smoothly. When adding a carpet after your child has started school, choose a color that blends with the existing design scheme, unless you are redecorating the entire room.

Paint
Your child may enjoy having pathways, stripes, a map, game board, free-form geometric design, or a solid-color painted floor.

It is not difficult to paint a wood floor, but before you start make sure it is clean, smooth, and dry. Sand any rough spots or splintered areas, and fill gaps and cracks with appropriate wood putty. Use a primer on the floor first. Then, tape off any designs or draw them with a soft-lead pencil. Use any good oil-based or enamel paint for the finished color. (Paint made specially for floors and decks covers well, but it comes in a limited range of colors.) Start painting in the corner farthest from the door and work toward the door. When dry, coat the floor with polyurethane for extra protection.

Stenciling. Applying stencils on a painted or natural wood floor offers additional design possibilities for the entire floor, parts of the floor, or only around the perimeter. (Stencils can be purchased at a hobby store, or you can make your own—see How To Stencil Floors, opposite page.)

If the floor plan is complex, remember to keep the rest of your design fairly simple and to keep other colors neutral if you want the floor to be the center of attention. Any design or colors painted on the floor can be continued as a motif throughout the room.

How to Stencil Floors

Stenciling is an easy, inexpensive way to add interest to large unadorned areas such as the floor. To make your stenciling look crisp and professional, practice on scrap wood or paper until you are comfortable with the technique.

1. Prepare the work surface to be stenciled. Measure and draw guidelines on the surface to keep the design placement even.
2. To make your own stencil, trace the design onto clean art board. Or, draw your design directly on art board. Place heavy acetate over the completed image. (Use the same size of acetate for all your stencils to make placement and spacing on the stencil area easier.) Tape acetate and the completed image together and place them on a suitable cutting surface, such as heavy cardboard or scrap wood. Hold a sharp mat knife securely at a 90-degree angle and cut toward you, turning the design as needed. Cut out only the areas that will be painted the same color. Continue to trace, tape, and cut until you have a separate stencil for each color or each shape.

3. Use masking tape to secure a stencil to the surface. Use a stencil brush or sponge to lightly paint through the openings of the stencil. The paint applicator should be very lightly coated—almost dry. Dab off excess paint before stenciling to avoid drips and built-up edges. Remove the stencil carefully, and wipe it off to keep the cutout edges crisp and clean, and to avoid smudges. Continue until you have stenciled the entire area in that color.
4. When the paint is dry, position another stencil over the incomplete design to add the second color, the third color, and so on. Protect the finished design by covering the surface with a clear, mat polyurethane varnish.
5. Add highlights and finishing touches with a small paintbrush.

Stenciling Technique

1.

2.

3.

4.

This painted and stenciled floor looks like an elaborately woven rug. The background color coordinates with the wall treatment, and the accent colors reflect the furnishings.

Walls and Ceilings

Even children have a sense of order and design, and they will certainly appreciate your help in complementing their room with touches that reflect their own style as well as that of their family.

At first the walls of their rooms provide children with a sense of security. Later the same walls give them privacy. At all stages wall treatments can provide visual stimulation and contribute to the feeling of the room.

Paint

White paint makes a suitable background for colorful toys, posters, and just about any design. For an infant's or toddler's room, you might want to start with white glossy paint. It's washable, can be easily touched up every few years, and can make a room seem larger since it reflects light. Details such as moldings, panels, and doorknobs can be painted a different color to add interest.

Instead of white walls, you might choose colors that complement those of the furnishings, or you might decide on colorful walls with a white ceiling. There is a vast array of color combinations you can select. Don't limit yourself to what is fashionable. Let your child's personal taste be your guide. Color combinations for large areas such as walls and ceilings should be worked out on paper before making final decisions. Make a scale drawing of the room with approximate furniture selection and placement. On tissue overlays, fill in areas with your color choices. This will give you an approximation of how the large painted areas will affect other features of the room.

Decorative Molding

Dividing the walls into upper and lower sections adds interest to a room. To do this, make a chair rail, or dado (a decorative strip of wood molding). The molding can have

hooks for hanging clothes and toys, or it can be used to exhibit a young child's art or as a kind of bulletin board for tacking up clippings, notes, etcetera. Upper and lower sections can be painted different colors, or one section can be covered with wallpaper, a design, a mural, or a frieze.

Still another alternative is to use the lower section of the wall for drawing. Children love art activities, and walls are an inviting canvas for them.

Top: The color in this small room makes it look lively without appearing to decrease its size.
***Above:** A chair rail divides the wall and can be used to hang playthings at child level.*
***Above left:** A view of the opposite side of the room at top shows how color and structure demarcate sleep and work areas.*

Top: *Simple geometric designs in bright colors are a dramatic and easy way to liven up walls.*
Above: *Stenciled designs add splashes of color to a small-print wallcovering.*

Some white walls can be treated so that children can draw on them with crayons and felt-tipped pens. The drawings can then be wiped off. (Be sure your child understands that this is not to be done to the other walls in the house.)

Supergraphics

Using supergraphics is another creative way to liven up a wall or define play and sleep areas. Instead of painting a mural, paint (or cut out from fabric or plywood and attach) huge numbers, the letters of your child's name, a giant protractor, ruler, or other objects. (For preschoolers, numbers and letters have the added advantage of being educational.) Trace silhouettes of members of your family onto a white wall and paint the figures in with bright colors or in black for a particularly dramatic effect. Use strips of light-tack masking tape spaced apart on the wall to create a pattern of lines of different widths. Paint the spaces between the strips of masking tape, and remove the tape gently when the paint is dry.

Wallcovering

If you use wallcovering as part of your design, remember that it will serve as a background for everything in the room and that furnishings should reflect the pattern or coordinate with it. Wallcovering for an infant's room should have a pattern that isn't overwhelming. If you don't choose a type that can be wiped clean (washable vinyl or self-adhesive plastic are practical choices), you can give it one or two coats of mat polyurethane for protection, although it will probably yellow the surface a bit. (Do a test first to make sure colors won't run.)

Wallcovering with a large design will usually make a room seem smaller, and covering with a small design will tend to make a room look larger; however, the opposite can hold true with intentional and selective use of color and pattern. But, be aware that it will take careful planning and foresight to accomplish the desired effect.

For interesting effects, try using diluted white glue to paste comic pages, magazine covers, or posters to the wall, and then protect them with polyurethane. Keep in mind that wallcovering can be applied to ceilings, too.

Fabric

Fabric can look luxurious and can warm up a space. It is also a good choice for sound absorption in a noisy room. Fabric of the same pattern used throughout a room makes it look cohesive. For variations on the basic pattern, add a pattern in a smaller or larger scale, or one with the same pattern but in two different colors. Washable fabrics are the best choices.

Appliques and Indian cotton spreads make good wallcoverings, and a whole ceiling can be draped or tented with fabric. A king-sized bed sheet taped with fabric adhesive, hung, or stretched and stapled to a wall, provides a colorful background that can be easily changed.

When working with fabric or any design element, consider pattern and texture. A pattern (any repeated shape) has a textural quality, and textures create their own patterns, so avoid inadvertently creating too many patterns—the overall effect can be chaotic.

Trompe l'oeil

You might want to try your hand (and eye) at adding a trompe l'oeil effect. For example, in a room without windows, your child would probably enjoy having a false window painted on the wall. The window might have birds and plants on the windowsill look out over a garden, or have characters from your child's favorite story looking in. A trompe l'oeil picture frame might be used to display some real art, or a real-looking rabbit hole could be behind an actual table set for a tea party.

Above: Patterns and textures of carefully chosen fabric and accessories all work together to create a charming effect in this girl's room.
Right: Picture rail molding defines a space ideal for applying a graphic frieze.

Murals

One way to decorate walls is by painting murals. Paint simple shapes and figures, or use your imagination to transform a room into a seascape, outer-space vista, zoo, jungle, or a scene from a fairy tale. Use the wall to show a skyline or to tell a story. The mural doesn't have to be restricted to walls; it can incorporate objects, moldings, and architectural features; extend upward from the floor, over the doors, and onto the ceiling; and incorporate furniture that is painted as part of the scene. The ceiling can be treated as a separate mural, perhaps painted with clouds or a night sky. Complete the effect by hanging real kites, origami birds, model spaceships, or mobiles.

An easy way to create a mural is to make a photographic slide of a design you want to reproduce. Simply project the mural on the blank wall and trace the outlines. If you are creating an original design, draw your mural on a sheet of paper divided into a grid of ½-inch or 1-inch squares. Draw a large version of the grid, consisting of the same number of squares, on the wall. Using a pencil or colored chalk, transfer the outlines one square at a time. Finally, paint the mural (oils and acrylics work well), working top to bottom so you won't be standing over wet paint. Fill in all the areas that need one color (painting large areas first), then wait for the paint to dry before filling in the next color. Murals can be protected with a coat of mat or satin polyurethane varnish, which also accentuates the colors. When your child outgrows the mural, it can be painted over.

Windows

Window treatments, like wall treatments, can be plain or decorative, and changed easily as your child matures. A window treatment can give a room character, establish a motif, or become the basis of a design for the rest of the room. Whatever treatment you choose should be easy to clean and appropriate for your child and your lifestyle.

Blinds

A practical choice for window coverings are blinds of one sort or another. They are safe and easier to clean than curtains. They control light efficiently and can be color coordinated with the rest of the room. Types of blinds include the popular miniblinds (with narrow slats that fit neatly on or in window frames) and venetian blinds, made of metal, plastic, or wood. Keep cords out of reach of toddlers.

Shades

Roller shades are another practical choice. They can allow full, partial, or little light. Shades are available in a variety of colors, designs, and textures. They can also be personalized by gluing on decorative fabric or wallpaper cutouts or by painting them. In the nursery black-out shades or cloth shades with a silver backing protect babies from the morning sun and help them sleep during the middle of the day. For older children bamboo, matchstick, and woven wood shades are inexpensive and decorative, although they allow some light to come through.

To create an unusual window treatment, try hanging rows of hats, panels of lace, mobiles, models, or chimes in front of a roller shade. If privacy isn't an issue, use these items to filter the light without the roller shade behind them.

Fabric

Window coverings made out of fabric are soft and appealing. They are not the most practical choice for a child's room, but they are easy to make, can fit any sized window, and can be coordinated with other fabrics used in the room. It is best to keep curtains short, such as cafe-style curtains, so that toddlers don't pull on them and so they are out of the way during active play of older children. Lightweight washable fabrics work best in conjunction with roller shades, which control the light more effectively.

Window Treatments

Supergraphic on wall encompassing window frame and miniblind

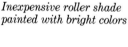
Inexpensive roller shade painted with bright colors

Decorative fabric treatment with matching roller shade

Mobile to filter light in front of roller shade

Door Treatments

Painted and stenciled door and wall

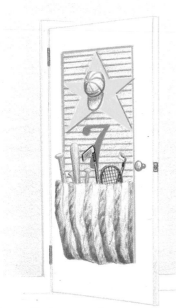

Door with storage pockets

Dutch door with graphics

Doors

Psychologists say that closed doors can make young children feel isolated. When treated in a colorful or humorous way, however, the same doors can become less forbidding. Try adding a trompe l'oeil painting that makes the door look like an entrance to an enchanted forest, or hang pockets with toys or a poster. Stencil the door, paint a super-graphic of your child's name, add a blackboard, or trace your child's shape and make a plywood cutout with hooks attached for hanging clothes in the right places. Another good idea, for young children, is a Dutch door, which turns the whole room into a sort of playpen. You can watch your children, yet they are confined to the safety of their room while you take care of other chores. For older children a bulletin board or cork panel attached to a door will also help soundproof it. (If you move often, hang the board from a flat-topped hook over the top of the door to avoid marring the surface.)

Not only is a door a good place for storage, it can be used as a backdrop for game equipment.

STORAGE

Baby carriers, dia-pers, books, dolls, bicycles, models . . . there never seems to be enough storage!

You'll soon have to find room for toys, clothing, and art materials. In a few more years you'll need space for educational playthings, hobbies, and books—not to mention outgrown toys. Sooner than you think, you'll have to accommodate school supplies, sports equipment, electronic games, and computer and audio-visual equipment.

Organization

The key to keeping the chaos down to a minimum is organization. Storing everything within easy reach will save you time and energy when children are infants and will encourage them to keep the room in order when they are older. Children like convenience too—when they can't find what they are looking for, they become frustrated and everything ends up in a heap. To avoid this, materials that relate to a particular activity should be located near where the activity takes place (even if you think the activity should take place someplace else). It won't help to store blocks in bins at one end of the room if your child plays with them at the other end. Toys and art supplies should be kept within your child's reach; anything that won't be used for a while or that needs adult supervision can be stored out of reach.

Preschoolers are able to learn many ordering skills. Ask your child to help you arrange belongings by similar size, shape, or color. Arrange items from biggest to smallest or by categories (all board games in one place, for example, and all puzzles in another). Older children might want to arrange their clothing by color or

function, such as dress clothes, play clothes, and school clothes. Decide together on a system for arranging the books (by subject, title, size or where they are read in the room). With the child's input, you will probably devise a plan that is workable and reinforces learning skills.

Built-in Storage
Space saving and attractive, built-in storage may be less expensive than freestanding furniture. Built-in units include cupboards, platforms,

An efficient one-wall design includes a bed, a dresser, a desk, and storage space—a decorative, open wall unit also uses the area above the desk for displays.

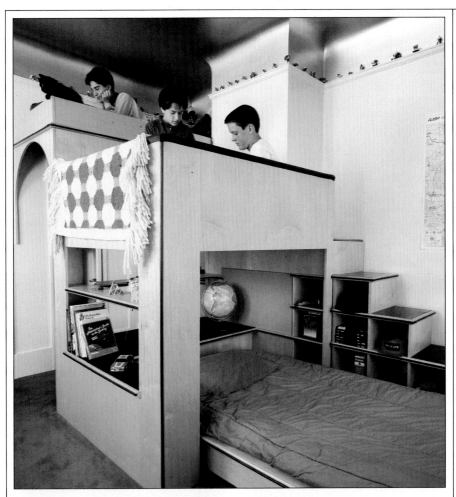

shelves, and bookcases. Storage can also be built in under windows in the form of a window seat. Since a window is a good source of natural light, the window seat can become a reading nook, play area, or study.

Don't overlook closets when considering storage space. When a closet is set up for easy use, it is less likely that things will get tossed in. Buy a storage system from a closet specialty shop or create your own system. Some steps for organizing and making the best use of closet space follow:

☐ Consider installing wire-basket systems, adjustable shelves, rods, or storage modules in the closet. Add shelves of different sizes along the sides or width, or put in tall cabinets. Stackable boxes, bins, drawers, and special hangers can all add usable space to a closet.

☐ Find out whether your child can easily reach necessary objects already in the closet. If space below the clothes pole is being wasted, lower it for greater accessibility and to gain room on top. During the early years poles may not be necessary at all since most clothing lays flat. Later, you can add a clothes pole mounted low enough so children can hang up clothes themselves.

☐ If the closet is bursting at the seams, make two lists: one of things that no longer need to be kept there and a second of things that need to be in the closet, such as clothes, rainwear, sports equipment, and current games. Discuss with your child how things might be organized so they can be found and reached easily. Label shelves and containers for young children.

☐ For an infant you might be able to use the closet as a changing room. A changing shelf and small shelves for linens, clothing, and toiletries can be built in.

☐ Don't forget the back of the closet door. Following are a variety of items that make use of door space: hooks, grids, bulletin boards or pegboards, a mirror, a towel rack, a shoe bag for holding toys, and hanging shelves.

Top: *This multifaceted structure combines play, study, storage, and sleep space in an efficient cube design.*
Above: *A small staircase doubles as storage space.*
Left: *A storage system installed in the closet helps maximize closet space.*

Open Storage

Storage can be practical and decorative and also encourages organization. When young children can see their toys and reach them, they are more likely to play with them; when they can see where toys belong, they are more likely to return them. (A toy chest is effective for school-age children but isn't as useful for younger children since they often forget about what isn't in sight.) Rows of bins, baskets, crates, and trays on shelves are all examples of open storage units that can be placed at child level. Open storage is a practical way to display the myriad of things that just about every child collects.

Small objects can be placed in organizers hung on the wall, large objects on open shelves. Displaying your child's collections will give the room warmth and personality, but be careful not to display so many items that the room looks cluttered (parts of a collection can be stored, and then displayed on a rotational basis).

Portable Storage

Improvised and portable storage is both inexpensive and practical. Storebought component systems provide flexible storage, and often come in bright colors. The colors can be used to form a color-coded system for helping toddlers and preschoolers organize. All green things might go into the green container and all yellow things into the yellow. Toys could be organized by the kind of toy, such as stuffed animals in the purple container, trucks in the red bin, figurines in the yellow bin, and so on.

By looking around supermarkets, flea markets, hardware stores, and your home and office, you can find improvised storage units and containers that can meet just about any need. Let your children help in the search, and as new toys are purchased or new collections started, ask how they would like them displayed or stored. On the following page you'll find a list to get you started. With a little ingenuity, you'll have no trouble coming up with ideas.

Above: *A built-in unit combines open and concealed storage for both everyday and long-term use.*
Left: *Open baskets are lightweight, easy to move, and provide child-level storage.*

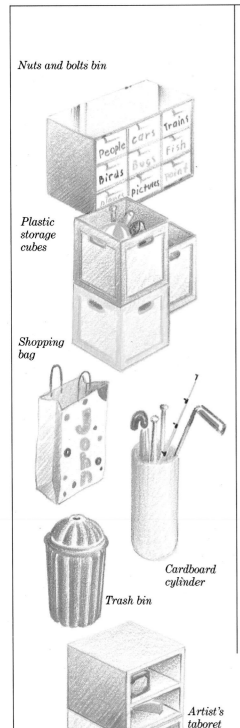

Nuts and bolts bin

Plastic storage cubes

Shopping bag

Cardboard cylinder

Trash bin

Artist's taboret

Stow It

Illustrated and listed on this page are a selection of inexpensive storage units and containers.

□ A variety of stacking plastic drawers, shelves, and cubes are easy to find at home improvement centers and hardware stores.

□ Organize papers in plastic and cardboard file boxes and filing cabinets (the tops can be used as work or play surfaces).

□ Small paper containers, large cardboard drums, boxes with cardboard dividers, cardboard take-out containers, and hatboxes can all be found either at home or at local stores. Sturdy boxes can be painted and have wheels attached to provide portable storage.

□ Leftover shoe boxes can be labeled and stacked. Spools or drawer pulls can be attached for use as handles.

□ Cutlery organizers and ice-cube trays are great for small items.

□ Baskets—hung, shelved, or on the floor—house countless belongings.

□ Storage units to be found at hardware stores include pails, plastic trash bins, mailboxes, toolboxes and tackle boxes, laundry baskets, and compartmentalized drawers and trays.

□ Hooks and pegboards can be installed to utilize wall space.

□ Plastic containers with lids and metal cans are great for stowing sports equipment.

□ Cardboard cylinders can be lined up, or glued together to form a cluster, then painted.

□ Drawer and bin units on casters, and roll-around taborets are favorite storage units.

Painted box put on wheels

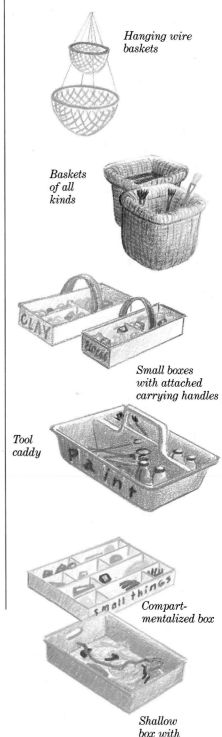

Hanging wire baskets

Baskets of all kinds

Small boxes with attached carrying handles

Tool caddy

Compartmentalized box

Shallow box with handles cut out

LIGHTING

An important element of design, lighting is also an element of function. Although the type and amount of light needed changes over time, it must be adequate and safe.

A nursery needs heavy-duty curtains or a black-out shade and general room light. Install a dimmer to create a constant reassuring glow that can be increased gradually during the night if your child wakes.

For toddlers and preschoolers, general room light can be provided by a ceiling or wall light. Avoid fluorescent fixtures, which cast a harsh light. Hang or mount all lights permanently; avoid table lamps, at this age, which can be knocked over. Do not exceed the recommended wattage for fixtures.

Older children need both general room light and lighting for specific activities. A central light (positioned where it is most needed) and a row of

spotlights or a side light and spotlight suspended from the ceiling are two ways to provide general light. Other possibilities for general room light include evenly spaced wall lights, recessed ceiling lights around the perimeter of the room, track lighting, and center-mounted ceiling lights. Track lighting is easy to install and can be adjusted to illuminate different areas at the same time, or change the mood of the room.

There are many types of lights available for study, reading, work, play, and storage areas. Gooseneck and drafting lamps are especially adaptable choices since they are easy to adjust. Low-hanging lights with wide-brimmed shades are good over a desk area, and a clip-on or shielded wall light is useful for reading in bed. For lighting a study desk for older children, combine an adjustable desk lamp with overhead lighting.

A bedside reading light is often a favorite room accessory for children who like to curl up with a book.

Types of Lighting

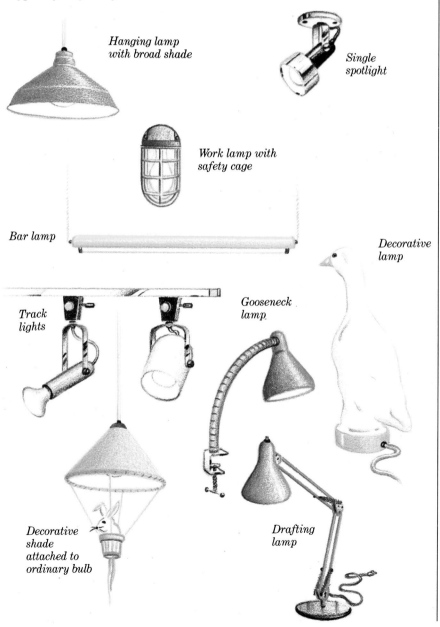

Hanging lamp with broad shade

Single spotlight

Work lamp with safety cage

Bar lamp

Decorative lamp

Track lights

Gooseneck lamp

Decorative shade attached to ordinary bulb

Drafting lamp

ERGONOMICS

I magine having to crawl around on the floor for a day. Now imagine sitting on chairs so high your legs can't touch the floor and having to stretch your arms to reach the top of the table.

If something you wanted was out of reach, you might give up in frustration or you might try climbing to get it. (If you were successful, you probably wouldn't bother trying to put it back.) These are some of the problems children encounter because of their size.

The chart on this page will help you create a comfortable, usable, and safe environment for your child. The chart shows the average reach a child has from a standing position, average heights for play tables and work benches, and the average heights a desk and a chair should be for children at each age. Of course, measurements vary with the age and size of each child and can be adapted for children with limited mobility.

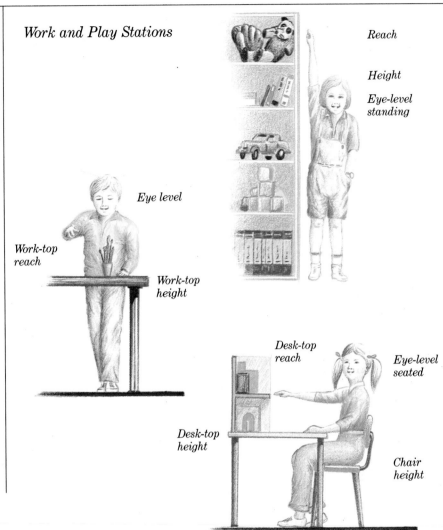

Work and Play Stations

Eye level

Work-top reach

Work-top height

Reach

Height

Eye-level standing

Desk-top reach

Eye-Level seated

Desk-top height

Chair height

Average Measurements for Work and Play Stations

Age	Child's Height	Eye-Level	Child's High Reach	Work-Top Height	Work-Top Reach	Desk Height	Chair Height	Eye-Level Seated	Desk-Top Reach
1	30"	27"	34"	18"	12"	12"	6"	19"	10"
2	35"	32"	39"	20"	13"	14"	7"	25"	11"
3	37"	34"	41"	21"	14"	15"	8"	27"	12"
4	39"	35"	44"	22"	15"	16"	10"	28"	14"
5	42"	38"	48"	23"	17"	17"	10"	29"	15"
6	45"	41"	52"	24"	18"	18"	11"	31"	16"
7	48"	44"	55"	25"	20"	19"	12"	34"	18"
8	50"	46"	58"	26"	21"	20"	12"	35"	19"
9	52"	48"	61"	27"	22"	21"	13"	36"	20"
10	54"	50"	65"	28"	23"	22"	14"	38"	21"
11	57"	53"	68"	29"	24"	23"	14"	39"	22"

FURNITURE

W hether designed and built by you or purchased, be sure furniture is durable and safe. There should be no sharp corners or rough edges; the pieces should be sturdy and, preferably, have washable surfaces.

If you decide to build your own furniture, you can have pieces that meet your exact needs and fit the spaces you have. You can also create furniture that is unique and imaginative. If you decide to buy furniture, you can have the convenience of pieces that are delivered to your home and ready to be used. Or, if you enjoy the hunt, look for used or unusual furniture items at the flea markets and garage sales.

Furniture that includes hidden storage (stools and tables with tops that lift off, beds with drawers below, etcetera) are wise choices if you are short on space. If you move often, furniture in neutral colors (white, beige, and wood tones) will go well with any decor. Avoid odd-shaped pieces that are difficult to arrange.

Shopping for Furniture

When shopping for furniture for infants and toddlers, buy pieces that can be lowered, raised, and added to—in other words, furniture that can be adapted for other uses at later stages. Avoid buying expensive nursery sets that will soon be outgrown.

As children get older, they will need comfortable chairs for relaxing and curling up in and sturdy chairs that provide back support while working. Preschoolers need some kind of table for art projects and games (wood or plastic tables, stacking tables, and reinforced cardboard-box tables can all serve both purposes), and school-age children need a desk or other surface to do schoolwork. Make sure the chairs, tables, and surfaces are sized for your child (see Ergonomics on page 45).

When buying a bed, be certain it has a firm mattress, and a protective railing for toddlers. You might want to choose a conventional twin bed with a box spring and mattress, a cut-to-fit foam slab, a platform bed with storage below, a trundle bed, or a loft bed. A mattress and plywood sheet suspended from the ceiling or a hide-away bed can be used to provide extra floor space.

A bunk bed is an obvious choice if you have two children or want an extra bed. The design of some bunk beds incorporates shelves and storage spaces attached upright to the bunks or below the lower bunk. Other designs provide hooks and rods on the frame for hanging clothes and surfaces for bulletin boards. Bunk beds can be designed in imaginative shapes (a double-decker bus, two Tootsie-Roll candies, a castle) and can later be split up into individual beds for use in separate rooms. With the addition of bright colors and graphics, and a fanciful head-, foot- or sideboard, individual beds can become racing cars, boats, or anything else you or your child can imagine. Bunk beds make good play areas, too. Attach a roller blind or curtains to the side edge of the top bunk to enclose the lower bunk and create a reading nook or playhouse.

When buying bunk beds be certain they are sturdy; easy for children to climb; and have a strong safety rail on the top unit, enough headroom for an adult to sit on the lower bunk, and good mattresses.

Unfinished Furniture

Unfinished furniture comes in a wide range of styles and is usually a good value. Some types can be customized by choosing from different hardware and finishes. Lower-priced pieces are

Top: A child's room is an ideal place for painted furniture.
Above: When buying or refinishing used furniture, be sure to repair any broken or chipped corners and edges that could produce splinters.
Opposite: A mix of custom-built furnishings, storebought storage, and furniture from around the house make this room inviting and functional.

generally made of soft white pine and look best when painted or finished. These pieces often use fiberboard sides and bottoms, nailed frames, and stapled drawers. Although not sturdy, this type of furniture can work well for a few years. Medium-quality furniture offers solid construction and is often made of knotty pine, maple, or birch. Top-quality hardwood furniture is sturdy and usually made of solid oak or cherry and has superior detailing. You can finish it with a variety of stains and finishes.

Used Furniture

Secondhand furniture is less expensive than fully finished new pieces, usually offers good quality, and can be refinished in whatever way you choose. Don't forget about old furniture you might have stored away. Unusual pieces, such as doctors' cabinets and display cases, can make good decorations and provide extra storage space.

Sources for secondhand furniture include estate sales, antique shops, yard and garage sales, auctions,

church bazaars, and the classified ad sections of newspapers, to name just a few. When buying used furniture, check the following details: Do the joints creak? How are the legs of chairs and tables attached and braced? How are the drawers put together and finished? Are nails exposed? Do drawers and doors open and close smoothly? Is hardware securely fastened? Are surfaces splinter-free? If any problem exists, be sure to repair the item before it is put to use in your child's room.

PROJECTS
YOU CAN
BUILD

*I*n this section you will find original furniture designs for children of three age groups: infancy (0 to 3 years), preschool (3 to 6 years), and school aged (6 to 11 years). Featured here are the key design structures in a child's room: the sleep, work and play, and storage areas. The creative and efficient projects illustrated in this chapter will provide your child with an environment that is inviting and responsive. The projects offer a variety of features and uses and a range of structural complexity. They have been selected to provide you with a cross section of ideas that will accommodate your child's changing needs plus your budget and carpentry skills.

Jorie, age 9
Clearlake, Illinois

AGES AND STAGES

T he overall changes that a child goes through in the first 12 years of life are astounding. From a completely dependent, nonverbal baby emerges an independent, agile, and articulate child capable of thinking on an abstract level, forming lifelong friendships, resolving moral conflicts, and perfecting a myriad of specialized skills.

The child's room undergoes metamorphoses in tandem with the occupant. Anticipate changes in scale, furniture, decoration, color, and materials—especially in the sleeping, working, and playing departments.

Physical Development

For all children physical development is a sequential shift from general to specific abilities and skills. The timing of the transitions from one stage of development to the next varies with each child, however. Because the timetable of development is individualized, age demarcation presented with ideas about the design and furniture size in a child's room is somewhat arbitrary. In discussions of size, however, the generally agreed upon averages make a convenient starting point for physical measurements (see the ergonomics chart on page 45). Just remember that they are only averages. Taking measurements yourself is the only way to know what size furniture would really fit your child. Similarly you must be the judge of when your child is ready to move from a crib to a railed bed or sleep without a guardrail, or when he or she needs a more sophisticated design style.

Sharing the Experience

While you're building a project for your child's room, it might be a good time to share your woodworking knowledge. Obviously, children should not use hand tools without adult supervision and lessons, and adults should always keep children at a safe distance from power tools. Children can, however, learn to measure, mark, follow plans, select screws, and help out in a variety of ways that are fun and educational. (Note: When you're working with tools, there should always be another adult present to supervise the children; you can't concentrate on tool handling and safety if you are also responsible for watching children.)

Tool Safety

Children learn much by example, and making an effort to use your tools safely reinforces what you teach them about tools. This list of reminders presents tips about tool safety that you will want to teach by example.
☐ Wear safety goggles whenever there is a chance of flying particles, whether working with hand tools or power tools. Use hearing protectors when your work produces noise.
☐ Do not wear loose clothing, which could catch in power tools. Footwear should be comfortable but sturdy. Wear gloves when handling wood but not when operating power tools.
☐ Be sure you understand the function of each tool and the way it is supposed to be used before you operate it. Read all instructions carefully; practice on scrap wood and proceed slowly.
☐ Pay close attention to what you are doing. A slip in concentration could result in the slip of a board or a hand.
☐ Keep your workplace neat and dry to avoid accidents.
☐ Be sure to unplug electric tools when they are not in use or when you are changing bits or blades.
☐ Keep cords out of the path of blades and drill bits.
☐ Use double-insulated plugs, proper wiring, and heavy-duty extension cords that have grounded connections. Always repair frayed cords immediately.
☐ Take time to think through all the procedures before you begin, and set up your work space accordingly.
☐ Never take safety for granted.

Selecting Projects

As noted in the previous chapters, one child's response to environment, people, and events may be quite different from another's, and the intensity and expression of the response may be just as variable. Keep the attributes of the specific child in mind when selecting projects to build for his or her room, and modify them to fit special needs. Discuss the project with children who are old enough to do so, and find out if they have color preferences or any design changes they would like to make.

The projects that follow have been designed to be safe, useful, and durable as well as to appeal to the builder and to the user. But remember, no matter how well a project is designed and built, there is no substitute for adult supervision when it comes to safety.

There are three project sections: zero to three years, three to six years, and six to eleven years. Each section starts with a brief description of the developmental tasks accomplished by children of the specified age group, and each of the projects corresponds to the developmental stage of that particular age.

Making a generalization about child development is a little like trying to hit a moving target, but the generalizations do provide a useful reference point for determining the suitability of a particular project.

IN THE BEGINNING
Newborn to Three Years Old

During the first three years of life, infants are learning to coordinate their bodies and to make sense of the world around them.

When babies enter the world, they cannot even hold their heads up, but within three years they walk, climb, grab objects, and make block towers.

Attachment

Newborns cannot distinguish one person from another. It takes time for them to develop bonds with caregivers. By the age of two, they have formed deep attachments and trust in their family members. Consistent, reliable care ensures that the newborn develops a sense of trust. The ability to trust enables the infant to tolerate frustration and not always require immediate gratification of desires.

Studies have shown that infants like small spaces, where it is believed they feel secure. Many also believe that rocking aids emotional development (the studies of this matter are inconclusive). A cradle, gently rocking carriage, or baby sling worn by an adult provides movement that seems desirable and enjoyable for young infants. But it's unnecessary to rush out and buy expensive infant furniture to fill this need; remember, it will be used for a very short time.

The focal point of a small and secure sleeping area can be a cradle, a bassinet, or even a basket. Consider making the handsome cradle on page 52, an heirloom piece that is easy to build. The crib for newborns on page 54 may have a short life as a crib, but becomes an attractive serving cart when crib rails are removed.

Colorful toys, wall treatments, and mobiles (which should hang 8 to 10 inches from the baby's eyes) can keep your infant occupied and stimulated for long periods. Babies see slow-moving objects and high-contrast colors better than they see stationary objects. Faces seem to be preferred objects; even a simple line drawing of a happy face can keep a newborn amused.

Independence

Infants soon become curious about their surroundings and are eager to experiment. Access to a variety of sensory stimuli encourages children to take the initiative. Encourage and amuse your child with musical toys, mirrors, objects with unusual textures, and open shelving for storing toys within sight.

Because toddlers are small, shelves for toy storage and furniture such as a table and chairs need to be low enough for them to reach into or climb upon unassisted. A small toy box on wheels (see page 58) is particularly appealing because toddlers can use it to pull themselves up when practicing walking and then push it to different places.

About the time that infants start to walk, they begin to show some self-direction. Although they have a strong desire for autonomy, they possess little judgment about their own capabilities. Adult supervision is required constantly for this age group, even in the "safety" of the home. Infants need to be protected from excesses as they randomly, but purposively, explore and begin the art of playacting. Once toddlers are secure with their sense of autonomy, they are capable and ready to play an active role in planning their activities.

Safety. When thinking about ground-level activities, you must always be aware of what is available to your youngster—electric outlets that need covers, windows and doors that need guards, and small objects that could be swallowed.

It is fascinating to watch children progress from one stage of development to the next.

ROCKING CRADLE

*T*he first few months at home with the new baby are so special that it's worth planning ahead to build an attractive cradle. This cradle—with an easy-to-build, elegant design—will serve for years to come, providing the soothing, rocking motion that babies love.

This cradle is designed to accept an 18-inch by 36-inch mattress, a standard size that is widely available. However, before building, make sure that this size is available in your area. If not, scale the cradle design up or down to suit your needs.

Remember that as soon as the baby is able to sit up unassisted (usually after four or five months), it's time to start using a full-size crib.

1. From a 4 by 8 sheet of ¾-inch birch plywood, cut 5 flat pieces for the ends, sides, and base of cradle. Bevel-cut base panel at 10 degrees.

2. Use the template shown to lay out patterns for cutouts on ends and sides. Drill ¼-inch holes as needed to give the saw blade room to maneuver, then cut out the shapes with a saber saw. Smooth all cut edges with a file, taking care not to splinter the surfaces of the plywood: Hold the file at a slight upward angle, and file toward the center of the cut, first from one side then from the other.

3. Cut 2 pieces of ¾-inch quarter-round to length and glue and nail them to one edge of each side panel. When glue is dry, cut 2 pieces of 1½-inch half-round to length and glue and nail them to the attached quarter-round. These will cover the exposed plywood edges and form rounded tops on sides of cradle.

4. Mark screw locations at 6-inch intervals along bottom edge of each side piece. Drill and counterbore holes for screws at a 10-degree angle so that screws will seat straight into bottom panel. Attach sides to base with glue and screws.

5. Lay end panels flat on the floor and set side-base assembly into position on each end piece. Note that sides attach to ends 1½ inches from edges. Trace shape of side and base onto end pieces. The penciled lines will guide you when drilling the pilot holes for the screws. Check each line—it should be parallel to closest side of the end piece. Make adjust-

ments if necessary in the screw locations; the base assembly can be flexed slightly to fit. Drill and counterbore holes at 6-inch intervals, through end into side, then screw end panels onto base assembly.

6. Bevel-cut two 12-inch pieces of 1 by 4 at a 45-degree angle on each end. Attach these braces underneath the cradle to connect end panels to base. Drill and countersink holes for 1-inch by No. 12 screws, then screw braces in place.

7. Plug or fill all screw holes, then sand cradle, rounding off all corners. Prime or seal all surfaces. Sand again before applying final finish.

Plan to have this enduring, classically styled cradle ready when the new arrival comes home.

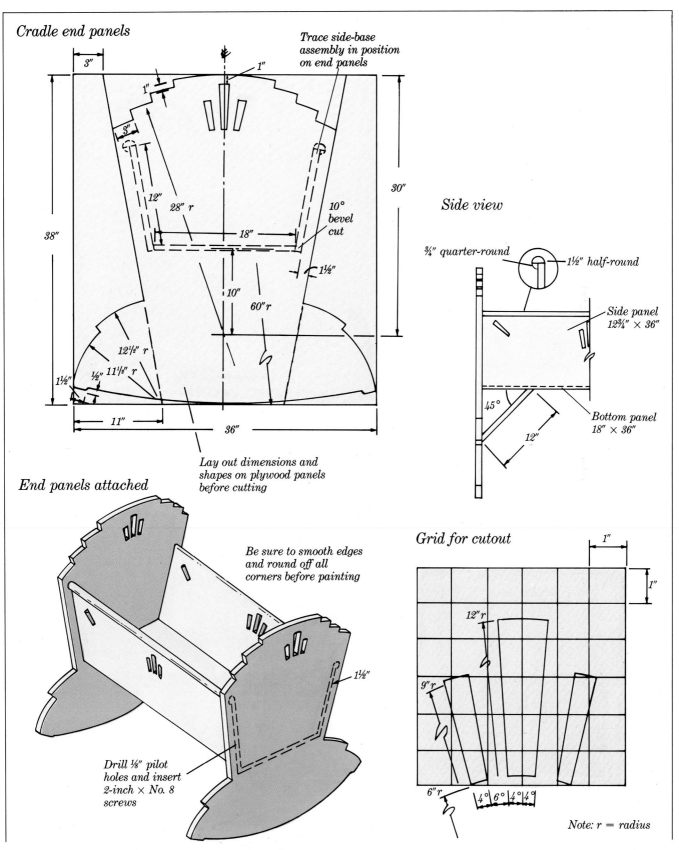

Cradle end panels

3"

1"

1"

Trace side-base assembly in position on end panels

3"

12"

28" r

18"

38"

30"

10° bevel cut

1½"

10"

60"r

12½" r

½" 11¼" r

1½"

11"

36"

Lay out dimensions and shapes on plywood panels before cutting

Side view

¾" quarter-round

1½" half-round

Side panel 12¾" × 36"

45°

12"

Bottom panel 18" × 36"

End panels attached

Be sure to smooth edges and round off all corners before painting

1½"

Drill ⅛" pilot holes and insert 2-inch × No. 8 screws

Grid for cutout

1"

1"

12"r

9"r

6"r

4° 6° 4° 4°

Note: r = radius

NEWBORN'S CRIB

*T*he unique feature of this crib is that it continues to be useful after the newborn graduates to a full-sized crib. Take the top rails and dowelled sides off, and the crib is transformed into an attractive changing table or cart. It can be kept in your youngster's room, but it's attractive enough to be used in the dining area, as well.

The woodworking techniques employed in this piece are fairly demanding—do not try it as a first joinery project. If you have some experience, however, you'll find it well within your capabilities. All joints are secured with glue and finishing nails unless otherwise specified.

Base Table Assembly

1. From 2 by 2 pine cut 4 legs 28 inches long. Mark points 3½ inches from top and 6 inches from bottom of each leg, then cut ¾-inch by ¾-inch dadoes across two adjacent faces of each leg.
2. Build upper and lower stretcher frames from 1 by 2 pine, with 45-degree miters at each end. Cut 4 pieces 32¼ inches long, and 4 pieces 17¼ inches long. Carefully crosscut ¾ inch off the mitered ends of each piece, then assemble pieces into frames in horizontal configuration. Cut and attach 5 evenly spaced 1 by 3 crosspieces inside upper frame. Glue four ½-inch-wide by 5/16-inch-tall strips to tops of second and fourth cross-boards to function as drawer guides.
3. Assemble legs onto upper and lower stretchers, taking care to main-

tain square as glue dries; use clamps if necessary. When dry, rout a stepped ¼-inch radius on edges that will surround side panels and drawer fronts.
4. From 1 by 4 pine cut two side panels to fit between legs. Also cut a 1 by 3 spine 29¼ inches long. Attach each side panel so that the outside is flush with inside of legs; center spine

and flush it with tops of side panels; glue in position and clamp until dry.
5. Out of ½-inch plywood cut a 32¼-inch by 17¼-inch piece to form the top. Drill pilot holes and countersinks, then glue and screw top to legs so that outer edges of legs are flush with corners of top. Apply laminate to top and trim with router using router bit. (For more on laminate, see page 82.)

You'll be using this newborn's crib long after the little one has outgrown it. Simply remove the crib rail and add casters, and the crib becomes an attractive serving cart for dining or living areas.

Base assembly

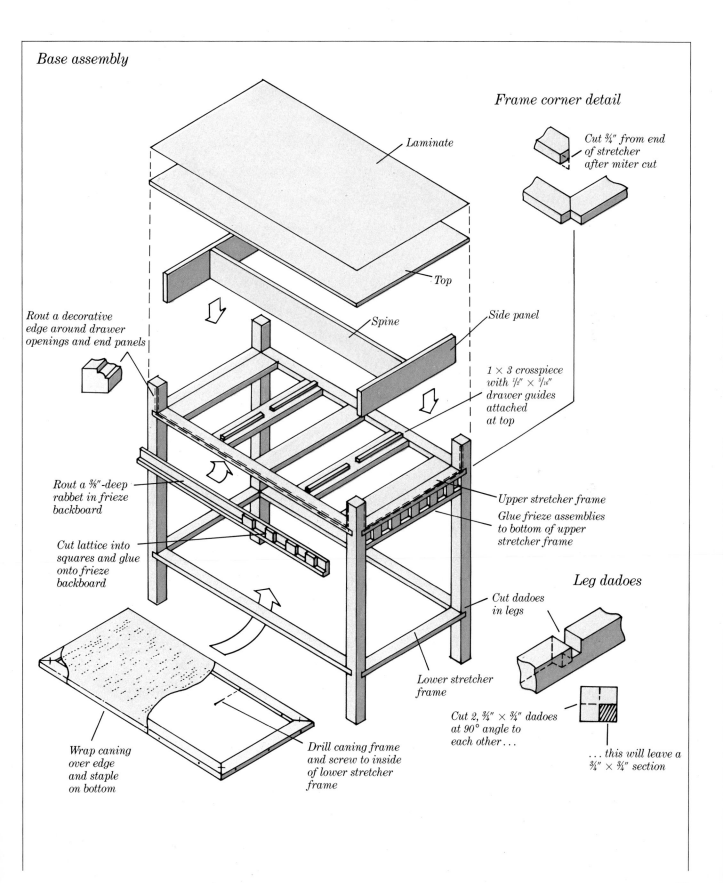

Laminate

Top

Spine

Side panel

Frame corner detail

Cut ¾" from end of stretcher after miter cut

1 × 3 crosspiece with ½" × 5⁄16" drawer guides attached at top

Rout a decorative edge around drawer openings and end panels

Rout a ⅜"-deep rabbet in frieze backboard

Cut lattice into squares and glue onto frieze backboard

Upper stretcher frame

Glue frieze assemblies to bottom of upper stretcher frame

Leg dadoes

Cut dadoes in legs

Lower stretcher frame

Cut 2, ¾" × ¾" dadoes at 90° angle to each other...

...this will leave a ¾" × ¾" section

Wrap caning over edge and staple on bottom

Drill caning frame and screw to inside of lower stretcher frame

6. Decorative frieze below drawers is constructed of lattice blocks glued onto a 1⅛-inch by ¾-inch back.

7. Build a frame from 1 by 2 stock to support caning. Make caning frame ⅛ inch smaller than opening between legs since caning will wrap around edges of frame before being inserted into base. Stretch dampened caning over frame and staple it to sides. Attach frame to inside of lower stretcher frame with 2½-inch by No. 6 flat-head wood screws driven from inner sides.

Drawer Assembly

Build 4 drawer boxes 3⁷/₁₆ inches deep, 14⁹/₁₆ inches wide, and 7½ inches long.

1. From ¾-inch stock cut front, sides, and back to sizes shown in illustration. Cut base from ¼-inch plywood. On inside of side pieces, rout vertical ¾-inch dadoes ½-inch from back edge. Cut 2 vertical ¾-inch-wide by ⅜-inch deep rabbets at each end of front panel. On sides and front pieces cut ¼-inch horizontal grooves ¾-inch from bottom edge.

From 1 by 2 stock cut 4 drawer guides 6¾ inches long. Center a ⁹/₁₆-inch wide by ½-inch deep groove lengthwise on 1 by 2 guides.

2. Using glue and ⅝-inch brads, assemble all drawer pieces as illustrated, except for drawer guides. When joints are set, apply a bead of glue to top (nongrooved) side of guides. Glue grooved guides to bottoms of drawers. Slide drawers into cabinet while glue is wet to assure alignment of guides as glue dries.

Crib Assembly

1. Cut ½-inch birch dowel into 64 pieces 9¾-inches long. For top and bottom segments of rail, cut 1 by 2 pine into 4 pieces 33 inches long and 4 pieces 18 inches long. Miter ends so they join in a vertical configuration.

2. Select 2 long pieces and 2 short pieces for top of rail. Rout a ¼-inch

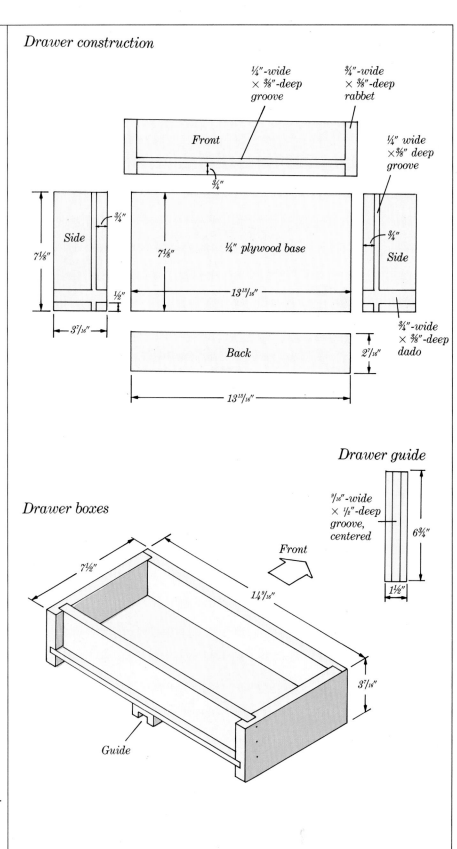

Drawer construction

¼″-wide × ⅜″-deep groove

¾″-wide × ⅜″-deep rabbet

Front

¼″ wide × ⅜″ deep groove

Side

7⅛″

¾″

½″

3⁷/₁₆″

7⅛″

¼″ plywood base

13¹³/₁₆″

¾″

Side

¾″-wide × ⅜″-deep dado

Back

2⁷/₁₆″

13¹³/₁₆″

Drawer guide

⁹/₁₆″-wide × ½″-deep groove, centered

6¾″

1½″

Drawer boxes

7½″

Front

14⁹/₁₆″

3⁷/₁₆″

Guide

stepped radius on outer edge of each piece. On 4 remaining pieces cut ³/₈-inch wide by ¹/₂-inch deep rabbets on what will be the lower inside edges.
3. Over full length of each of the 8 rail pieces, starting 1¹/₂ inches from end, mark center points for dowel holes at 1¹/₂-inch intervals. (Mark dowel holes on bottom face of upper rails and top face of lower rails.) Drill ¹/₂-inch holes ³/₈-inch deep in each of the center points.
4. Glue and clamp the 4 pieces of upper frame together. Drive a 1¹/₂ inch finishing nail through each side of each joint (see illustration); repeat for lower frame. When joints are set, apply glue to dowel holes in lower frame and set in railing dowels. To

complete railing assembly, glue and set dowels into upper frame.
5. Attach crib unit to top of Base assembly with 2 screws on each side of the bottom rail. Drill pilot holes 3 inches from each corner. Countersink and then drive 1-inch by No. 4 flat-head screws into pilot holes.

Finishing

1. When crib unit is no longer useful and is removed, you will need a decorative collar to cover plywood edges of the laminate top. Construct collar out of ³/₄- by ³/₄-inch stock. Cut

2 pieces 33 inches long and 2 pieces 18 inches long. Miter ends so they join in a vertical configuration. Cut ³/₈-inch wide by ¹/₂-inch deep rabbets on lower inside edges. Dowel and glue collar together.
    Store in a dry location until needed. Attach collar the same way as you did the crib railing (see step 5 of Crib Assembly, at left).
2. Finish wood as desired. The surface of the crib shown is distressed, stained, and shellacked.
3. Attach drawer pulls and, if desired, casters to bottom of legs. Make or buy suitable bedding. If you plan to use cart as a changing table after railing unit is removed, be sure to attach a safety strap.

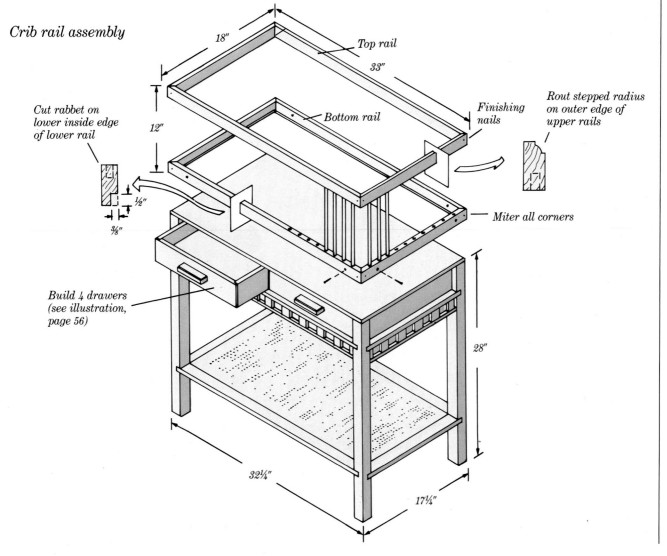

Crib rail assembly

18"

Top rail

33"

Cut rabbet on lower inside edge of lower rail

Bottom rail

Finishing nails

Rout stepped radius on outer edge of upper rails

12"

¹/₂"

³/₈"

Miter all corners

Build 4 drawers (see illustration, page 56)

28"

32¹/₄"

17¹/₄"

TODDLER'S STORAGE CART

In addition to serving as a seat, this rolling cart is the perfect place for stowing small toys and favorite objects.

This storage cart becomes the object of play as a child's imagination transforms it into a car, a grocery cart, or any kind of creation.

1. Out of ³/₄-inch stock cut 2 pieces 14 inches by 6³/₄ inches (front and back pieces) and 2 pieces 12¹/₂ inches by 6³/₄ inches (sides). Cut a 12¹/₂-inch square base out of ³/₄-inch plywood. Glue and nail pieces together. Set nails and round corners.

Screw a 12³/₈-inch long 1 by 1 to the inside of box front as shown to support the lid when closed. Use three 1¹/₄-inch by No. 6 flat-head screws to secure lid support.

2. Form a 12³/₈-inch wide by 12³/₈-inch deep lid from ³/₄-inch stock. If necessary, edge glue 2 boards together to make a single piece. When glue is set, trim piece to size and attach a 1 by 2 brace on underside.

3. To provide a hinge and lid support, glue and nail a 12³/₈-inch length of 1 by 2 on underside of lid, flush across back of lid. When glue is dry, round off back of lid to a semicircle and round edges of front and sides.

At rear of each side of lid, drill ¹/₈-inch pilot holes as shown. At front of lid, drill two ³/₈-inch diameter holes as shown and thread a length of clothesline through them so that ends are on underside. Tie knots at each end.

4. To build handle, cut 2 pieces of 1 by 2, each 19 inches long; cut 1 piece of 1⁵/₁₆-inch closet pole and 1 piece of 1 by 6 stock to 14¹/₈ inches long. Round off ends and edges, then using glue and finishing nails assemble pieces as shown in illustration. Drill a centered ¹/₄-inch hole, ³/₄ inch from bottoms of handle sides.

5. Out of 1⁵/₁₆-inch closet pole, cut 4 handle stops ⁷/₈ inches long. Glue and screw these to sides of box. Use 1¹/₂-inch by No. 6 flat-head screws. Fill and sand all pieces, then varnish.

6. Flip box over and screw 2-inch-diameter swivel casters onto base; inset about ¹/₄ inch from corners.

7. To position lid: Drill ³/₁₆-inch holes on opposite sides of box, 1⁹/₁₆ inches from back edge; 1¹/₈ inches down from top edge. Drive 3-inch by No. 10 flat-head screws through sides into lid.

8. To attach handle assembly: Drill ¹/₄-inch holes in sides of box, 1 inch up from the bottom and centered along side. Insert ¹/₄- by 2-inch flat-head machine screws through holes in handle assembly, placing a flat washer between handle and box. Secure screws on inside of box with flat washers and ¹/₄-inch locking cap nuts.

9. Be sure to buy and attach a center mount lid support that prevents the lid from closing unexpectedly.

A go-anywhere storage cart sized for toddlers adds variety to playtime. Toddlers will love to push, pull, sit on, climb on, and stow favorite playthings in this rolling cart. Don't be surprised when bigger kids want to join the fun, too.

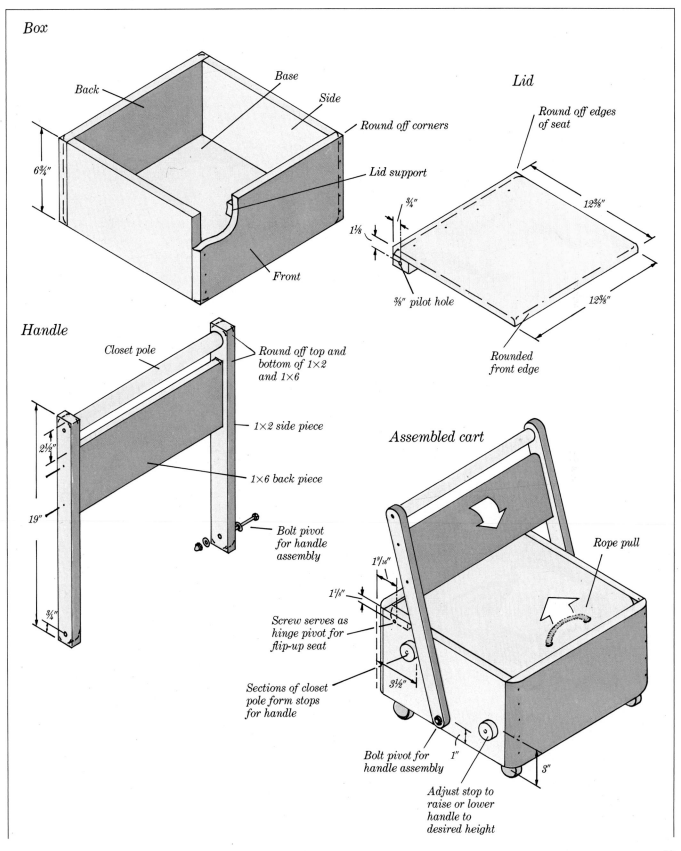

Box

Back

Base

Side

Round off corners

Lid support

6¾″

Front

Lid

Round off edges
of seat

¾″

12⅜″

1⅛

⅜″ pilot hole

12⅜″

Rounded
front edge

Handle

Closet pole

Round off top and
bottom of 1×2
and 1×6

1×2 side piece

1×6 back piece

Bolt pivot
for handle
assembly

2½″

19″

¾″

Assembled cart

Rope pull

1⁹/₁₆″

1⅛″

Screw serves as
hinge pivot for
flip-up seat

3½″

Sections of closet
pole form stops
for handle

Bolt pivot for
handle assembly

1″

3″

Adjust stop to
raise or lower
handle to
desired height

TODDLER'S TABLE AND CHAIRS

Here's a table and chair set that can grow with your children. Table legs are made of inexpensive plastic pipe, which can be easily replaced to change the height of the table. The sides of the chairs can also be easily replaced with taller sections.

1. Follow the diagram to make 1 sheet of ¾-inch plywood yield a 30-inch-square table, a chair with a back, and 2 small stools. (Remember to allow for the thickness of saw cuts when marking layout.)
2. Check pieces for fit, making sure chair stretchers equal width of seat minus thickness of sides. Carefully lay out stepped patterns on side rails of table, chair back, sides, and stretchers of stools and chair.
3. Using a piece of the plastic pipe as a guide, mark rounded corners of tabletop. With band saw or saber saw, cut rounded corners and stepped patterns. With table saw or radial arm saw, make 45-degree

bevels on ends of table rails and corner blocks.
   Drill counterbores and holes at 5- or 6-inch intervals around edges of tabletop and in chair pieces. Assemble as shown. Sand all pieces.
4. Cut table legs out of 1¾ inch plastic pipe. (You may want to cut the pipe an inch or two too long and adjust when table is assembled.) Sand all cut edges well. Lightly sand entire surface of pipe to ensure paint adhesion. (If different parts are to be different colors, paint pieces before assembly.)
5. To check that legs will fit correctly, screw rails to bottom of tabletop using 1½ inch by No. 6 flat-head wood

Children won't be bored when they have this brightly colored furniture that is fun yet functional to play on.

Cutting layout

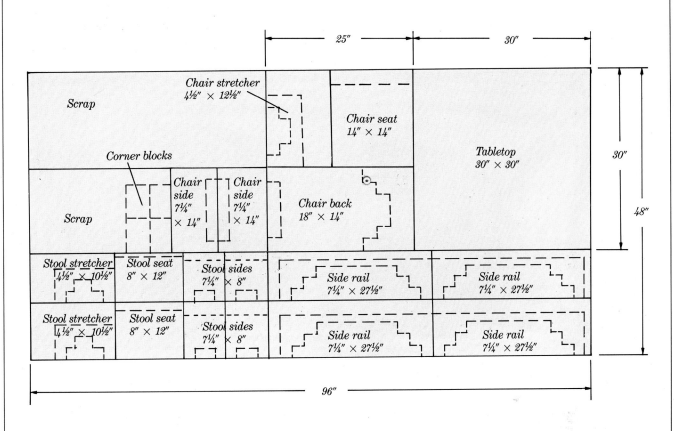

25″	30″		

Scrap

Chair stretcher
4½″ × 12½″

Chair seat
14″ × 14″

Tabletop
30″ × 30″

30″

Corner blocks

Scrap

Chair side 7¼″ × 14″

Chair side 7¼″ × 14″

Chair back 18″ × 14″

48″

Stool stretcher 4½″ × 10½″

Stool seat 8″ × 12″

Stool sides 7¼″ × 8″

Side rail 7¼″ × 27½″

Side rail 7¼″ × 27½″

Stool stretcher 4½″ × 10½″

Stool seat 8″ × 12″

Stool sides 7¼″ × 8″

Side rail 7¼″ × 27½″

Side rail 7¼″ × 27½″

96″

Table side rail

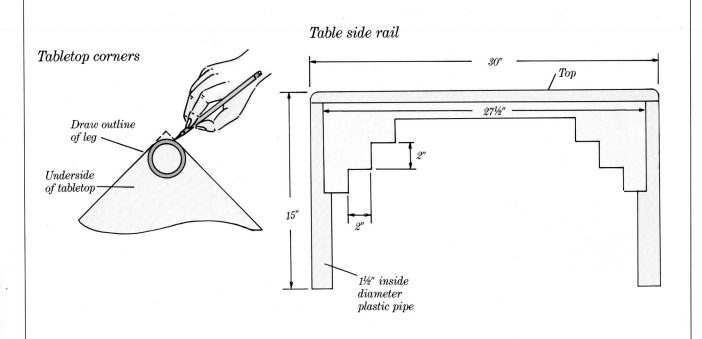

Tabletop corners

Draw outline
of leg

Underside
of tabletop

30″

Top

27½″

2″

2″

15″

1½″ inside
diameter
plastic pipe

Table

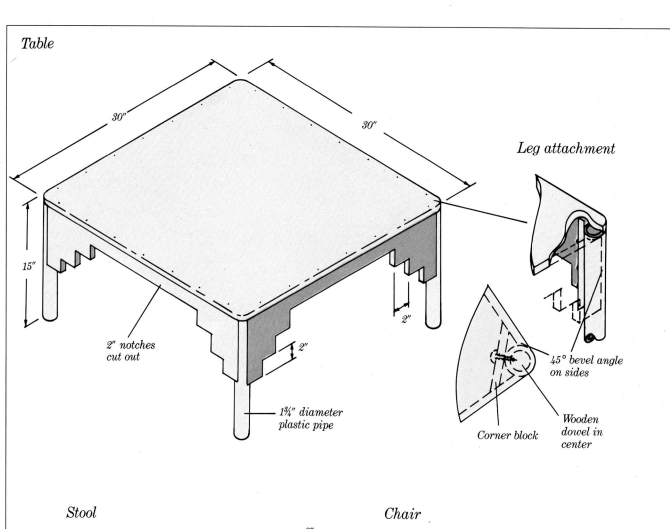

30"

30"

15"

2" notches
cut out

2"

2"

1¾" diameter
plastic pipe

Leg attachment

45° bevel angle
on sides

Corner block

Wooden
dowel in
center

Stool

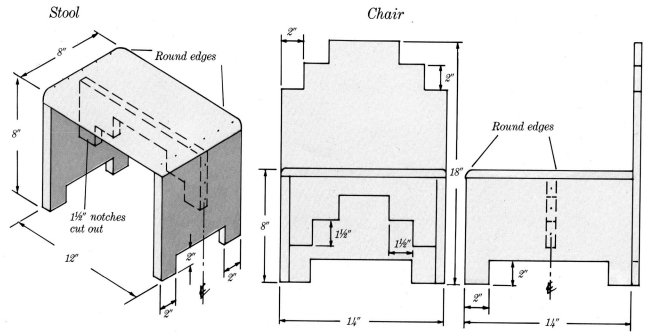

8"

Round edges

8"

1½" notches
cut out

12"

2"

2"

Chair

2"

2"

18"

8"

1½"

1½"

Round edges

2"

2"

14"

14"

Children enjoy the convenience of tables and chairs sized just for them. They can move about, reach, and sit comfortably without having to adapt their movements to adult-sized furniture.

screws or wallboard screws. Set tabletop upside down and line up one leg with rounded corner. Check fit of beveled corner block that attaches to the inside of rails at the corner. Adjust or recut until blocks fit snugly between legs and rails. Drill and screw corner blocks at inside corners of the table.
6. Drill braces and drive 1½ inch by

No. 10 sheet metal screws through braces into legs. (For a stronger corner, drive screws into a piece of wood dowel fitted inside the pipe.)
7. Unless painted earlier, give table a final sanding, prime, and paint.
8. Screw pieces for chair and stools together using 1½-inch by No. 6 flathead screws. Sand, making sure all edges are rounded. Prime and paint.

CHANGING TABLE

T*his easy-to-build project quickly changes a dresser top—no matter how shallow—into a changing table that you can make as deep as you want.*

1. Out of ¾-inch plywood, cut base piece 20 inches wide and as long as your dresser plus 1½ inches so that the sides of the changing-table top will slip over dresser top.

To cut slots that accommodate safety strap: Mark vertical centerline, and measure 5 inches in from each side. Drill and cut out 2 vertical slots 5 inches long and 1 inch wide. To provide clearance for strap, use a router to remove ⅜ inch of bottom surface between slots. When safety strap is threaded through slots, changing table will lie flat on the dresser top.

2. From 1 by 10 board, cut a backboard to the same length as base. Cut 2 end pieces; each should be 20⅜ inches long. Drill and cut out handles as shown in illustration. Round off front edges of sides.

3. Cut dadoes in end pieces and backboard 4 inches from bottom edges. Make dadoes ¾ inch wide and ⅜ inch deep. Cut a rabbet the same size at inside back edge of each end piece. Check illustration to see how pieces fit together.

4. Sand pieces and assemble, using waterproof glue and nails. Set and fill nail holes, sand again, and seal or prime. Finish with a nontoxic varnish or enamel paint. If you would like a plastic laminated changing surface, apply the laminate before assembly, remembering to adjust dadoes in sides and back.

5. Make a safety strap from any soft, sturdy fabric. Sew on Velcro fastening tape for a buckle and thread strap

through holes in base piece from the back. To the backboard of the changing table glue Velcro fastening tape on which to attach an array of colorful objects to keep your infant occupied.

6. Screw changing table to back side of dresser so that the holes will not be apparent when the changing table is removed.

Optional Attachment
Measure width of dresser exactly. Glue and nail 1 by 1 cleat to front underside of changing table to match width of dresser. Also measure from top edge of table to top of drawers to make sure cleat does not obstruct drawers.

Cleat will complete 4-sided rim underneath changing table to hold it in position without screws. To avoid tipping, be sure table does not overhang dresser more than 2½ inches.

Simply measure the top of the bureau or chest on which you wish to fit this convenient changing table and follow the easy-to-build instructions on this page. The changing table shown has solid oak sides and a laminate-covered base.

Changing table

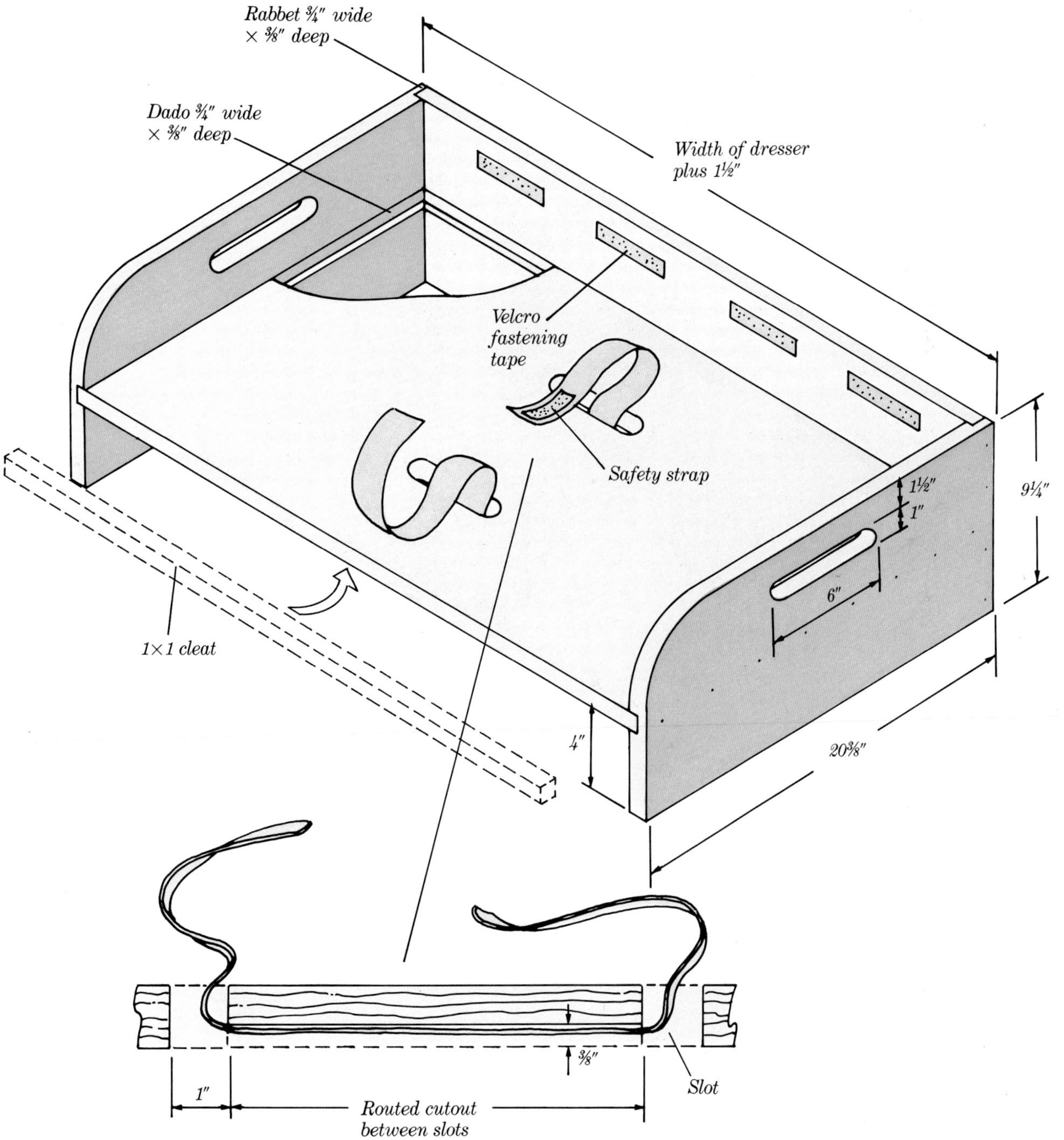

Rabbet ¾" wide × ⅜" deep

Dado ¾" wide × ⅜" deep

Width of dresser plus 1½"

Velcro fastening tape

Safety strap

1×1 cleat

1½"

1"

9¼"

6"

4"

20⅜"

⅜"

1"

Slot

Routed cutout between slots

Spend a little time and get a lot for your effort. This crib is two beds in one. It starts out as a crib and then converts to a bedroom set for a growing youngster. See page 70 for youth-bed conversion.

CRIB AND YOUTH BED

This versatile ensemble will serve a growing child from infancy through early teens. New drawer pulls and a change of color can make this bed sophisticated enough for a growing youngster.

As shown the beds are designed to hold standard mattress sizes—28 by 52 inches for the crib and 30 by 75 inches for the youth bed—but check

to make sure that you can obtain these sizes before you start to build.

This bed set provides ample storage. Initially, dressers rest on top of the youth bed, next to crib. When crib unit is removed, dressers come off, and can be placed separately in the child's room wherever needed. They can even serve as base units for a desk. Just paint a 24-inch by 80-inch flat door to use as a desk surface and mount it on top of dressers.

Drawers under the bed provide additional storage, but think about room configuration before building them. Will one side of bed be against a wall? If so, build drawers on only one side. Will the dressers be used as side tables at head of bed? If so, eliminate drawers at head of bed because side tables will impede opening and closing them.

Base/Youth-Bed Frame

1. From ¾-inch birch plywood cut 5 panels: 1 headboard 28 inches high by 33 inches wide; 1 footboard 21 inches high by 33 inches wide; 2 side panels 16 inches high by 75 inches long; and 1 base 31½ inches wide by 75 inches long.
2. Round upper corners of headboard and footboard as shown. (Make sure that footboard does not extend above height of crib mattress, since a young child could use it as a step to climb out of crib.)
3. Out of 2 by 2 material cut 2 side cleats 75 inches long and 2 end cleats 28½ inches long. Using glue and 2-inch by No. 6 screws, attach

Base assembly

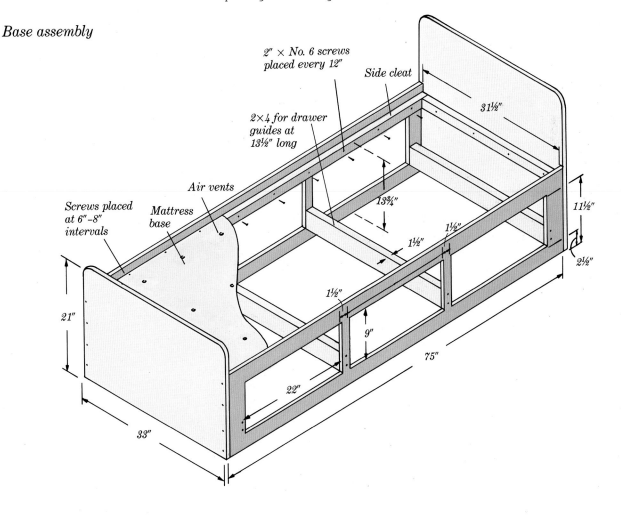

cleats to inside of side panels so that top edges of cleats are 13¾ inches above floor level as shown.

4. To lay out openings for drawers on side panels, measure up from bottom and draw 2 horizontal lines, one at 2½ inches and one at 11½ inches. Measure length of panel and mark centerline. Measure out 11 inches on each side of centerline and draw vertical lines that intersect horizontal lines to form a 22-inch-wide box for center drawer. Allow 1½ inches on each side of this opening, then mark another 22-inch-wide drawer on each side. (Remember that layout of these drawers is contingent upon room layout. Cut openings only for the drawers you plan to use.) Using a saber saw, cut out drawer openings.

5. Screw ends and sides together as shown. Drill pilot holes and use 2-inch by No. 6 screws.

6. To make supports for drawer guides, cut 4 pieces of 2 by 4 to 31½ inches long. Glue and nail these crosswise in frame so that bottom edges are flush with lower edge of drawer cutouts. Secure 2 by 4s with glue and 2-inch by No. 6 screws.

7. Attach mattress base to cleats with 1¼-inch by No. 6 screws placed at 6- to 8-inch intervals. To help ventilate bedding, drill ½-inch holes in base every 12 inches or so.

Drawer Construction

Before starting to build drawers for youth bed, purchase the drawer guides you will need. Select sliding roller-type guides in a length suitable for length of drawers you will build: 15 inches if you are installing drawers on both sides of bed; 20 to 24 inches if you will have drawers on only one side.

1. Read and follow directions supplied with drawer guides. Usually you will be instructed to build drawer boxes 1 inch narrower than the opening in order to allow ½ inch clearance on each side of box for guide.

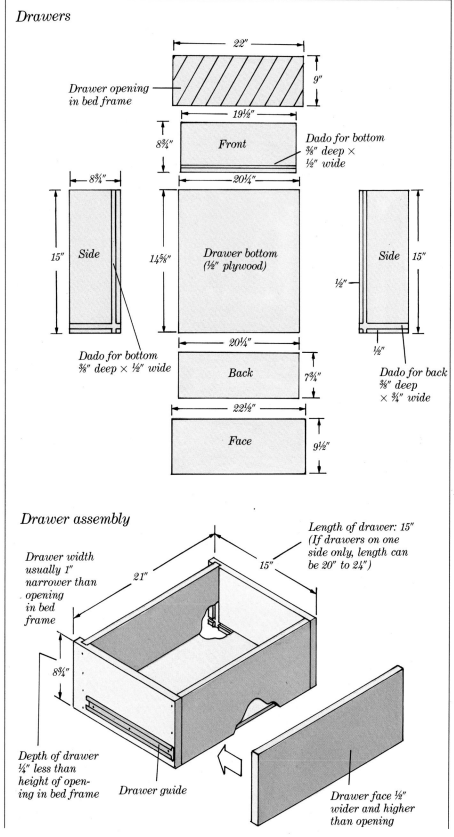

Drawers

Drawer opening in bed frame — 22" × 9"

Front — 19½" × 8¾"
Dado for bottom ⅜" deep × ½" wide

Side — 8¾" × 15"
Dado for bottom ⅜" deep × ½" wide

Drawer bottom (½" plywood) — 20¼" × 14⅝"

Side — 15", ½", ½"
Dado for back ⅜" deep × ¾" wide

Back — 20¼" × 7¾"

Face — 22½" × 9½"

Drawer assembly

Drawer width usually 1" narrower than opening in bed frame

21"   15"

Length of drawer: 15" (If drawers on one side only, length can be 20" to 24")

8¾"

Depth of drawer ¼" less than height of opening in bed frame

Drawer guide

Drawer face ½" wider and higher than opening

Taking this into account, start building drawers by cutting box fronts from ³/₄-inch stock. If drawer boxes are to be 21 inches wide (as shown in illustrations), make box fronts 19¹/₂ inches wide. Refer to illustrations for dimensions of all pieces, then cut sides, backs, and fronts to size out of ³/₄-inch stock. Cut base pieces out of ¹/₂-inch plywood.

2. Cut ³/₈-inch-deep dadoes in front and side pieces; space dadoes ¹/₂ inch from edges. Dadoes for drawer bases are all ¹/₂-inch wide and dadoes for backs are ³/₄-inch wide.

3. Using glue and ³/₄-inch brads, assemble drawer boxes as shown in illustration. Allow joints to set overnight. Attach guide assemblies to boxes and bed frame rails following manufacturer's instructions. Slide boxes into frame, check fit, and adjust guides as necessary. Position drawer faces on boxes so they overlap box front ¹/₄ inch on each side, mark locations, and remove boxes from bed frame. Glue face pieces

onto box fronts and drive four 1¹/₄-inch by No. 6 screws into drawer faces from inside drawer boxes.

Crib

1. Out of ³/₄-inch plywood cut mattress base to 33¹/₈ inches by 54¹/₂ inches. Cut three 1 by 3 boards for lower crib frame, but before attaching boards to plywood base, lay out and drill holes for dowel rungs. Refer to Crib Base Assembly illustration for dimensions of boards and layout of dowel holes. It is important to follow dimensions shown so that maximum space between rungs does not exceed 2³/₈ inches.

Inset boards ¹/₂ inch from edge of base; glue and clamp in place.

2. Drill ¹/₈-inch pilot holes through corners 1¹/₈ inch back from inside corner. (See illustration). Crib corner posts will be attached later.

3. From 1 by 2 stock cut one top rail to 32¹/₈ inches. From 1 by 3 stock cut remaining top rails: one at 53¹/₄ inches, one at 50 inches, two at 49⁷/₈

inches, and one at 32¹/₈ inches. Rip all 1 by 3 pieces to 1³/₄-inches wide, then cut rabbets for lap joints on each end of the 53¹/₄-inch rail and on one end of each of the 32¹/₈-inch rails.

4. Lay top rail pieces against their corresponding bottom rail pieces and transfer locations of dowel holes. Drill completely through bottom rails but only halfway through top rails in order to avoid exposed dowel joints on tops of rails.

5. Cut lengths of ³/₄-inch dowel: 26 at 27⁵/₈ inches; 17 at 15¹/₂ inches (for lower front dowels); and 17 at 11¹/₄ inches (for upper front dowels). Sand ends of dowels to facilitate assembly.

6. Assemble crib rail by first inserting dowels into holes in base, gluing and tapping with a mallet as you go. Next, glue top rails onto dowels, taking care to match lap joints at rear corners. Glue and clamp lap joints and let them set. Glue 11¹/₄-inch dowels and 49⁷/₈-inch rails together to form upper front (fold-down) rail assembly.

Crib assembly

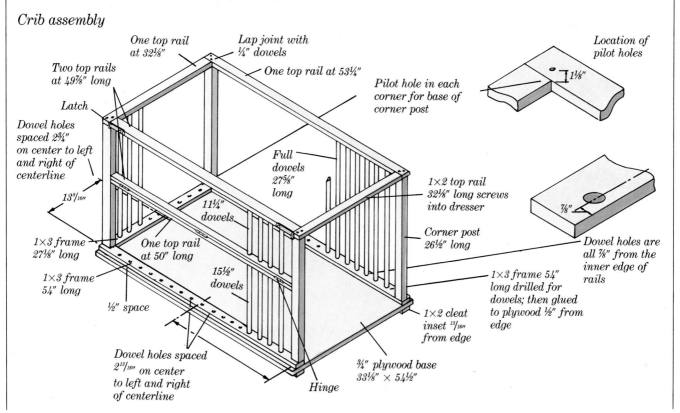

One top rail at 32¹/₈"

Lap joint with ¹/₄" dowels

One top rail at 53¹/₄"

Location of pilot holes

Two top rails at 49⁷/₈" long

1¹/₈"

Latch

Pilot hole in each corner for base of corner post

Dowel holes spaced 2³/₄" on center to left and right of centerline

Full dowels 27⁵/₈" long

1×2 top rail 32¹/₈" long screws into dresser

13⁹/₁₆"

11¹/₄" dowels

⁷/₈"

1×3 frame 27⁷/₈" long

One top rail at 50" long

Corner post 26¹/₂" long

Dowel holes are all ⁷/₈" from the inner edge of rails

1×3 frame 54" long

15¹/₂" dowels

1×3 frame 54" long drilled for dowels; then glued to plywood ¹/₂" from edge

¹/₂" space

1×2 cleat inset 13/₁₆" from edge

Dowel holes spaced 2¹³/₁₆" on center to left and right of centerline

¾" plywood base 33¹/₈" × 54¹/₂"

Hinge

Converted from the crib bed on page 66,
this youth bed and dresser set offers
plenty of drawer space for everyday and
long-term storage. This sturdy unit can
be set up in various configurations, and
the simple styling allows for easy color
changes over the years.

Cut four 2 by 2 corner posts to 26½ inches. Set in corner posts with glue and 2½-inch by No. 8 flat-head screws driven in from the bottom. Drill and dowel top corners with ¼-inch dowel, 2 dowels per corner. Carefully drill pilot holes into sides of front corner posts where top of lower rail assembly intersects. Secure each joint with two 2½-inch by No. 6 flat-head screws.

7. Attach folding railing assembly to top of lower front railing with three 1½-inch hinges, as shown in illustration. Install childproof sliding latch bolts at upper corners of folding railing. Finally, attach two 54½-inch 1 by 2 cleats to underside of crib base. Inset them ¹³/₁₆ inch from edges.

Dresser

Instructions given are for one of the two dressers shown in photograph. Repeat steps to build second unit.

1. From ¾-inch birch plywood cut top and bottom panels 20½ inches by 16⁹/₁₆ inches. Cut side panels 26½ inches by 16⁹/₁₆ inches. Using glue and finishing nails, assemble these pieces into a case with top and bottom overlapping sides. Measure and cut a back to fit within case.

Glue back to sides, then drive finishing nails from the outside every 4 inches. Cut an 18-inch cleat out of 1 by 2 and attach to bottom, positioning it ¹³/₁₆ inch back from front edge and centered between sides.

2. Install 3 drawers in case by first measuring opening into which they will fit. Opening should be 19 inches wide by 26½ inches high. After subtracting 1 inch (or amount specified by manufacturer) to account for drawer guide hardware, drawer boxes should be 18 inches wide. The 26½ inch height allows for 3 drawers: the top one 6⅜ inches deep, the bottom two 9¼ inches deep. Using these dimensions and a length of 14 inches, build boxes in manner described on page 68. Remember to make each drawer box approximately ¼ inch shorter than height of opening so they will not bind.

3. Fit guide hardware onto boxes and into case. Check fit of boxes and adjust as necessary. Attach a face panel cut from ⅜-inch stock to front of each drawer box, carefully measuring and cutting panels to overlap front edges of case by ⅜ inch.

4. To finish exposed plywood edges at top and bottom, apply veneer tape; or, if you will be painting units, fill and seal edges before painting.

Assembling Finished Units

1. Before fitting component pieces together, fill and sand entire project, taking care to round over sharp edges and corners. Then apply a nontoxic, child-safe finish.

2. When finish is dry, install drawer pulls on all drawers. Set crib onto "foot" end of youth bed. Cleats on mattress base will keep it in place.

Remove drawers from dresser units and, reaching inside, join dressers back to back with six 1½-inch by No. 6 flat-head screws. Set joined dresser unit onto youth bed and replace drawers. End of dresser unit serves as one end of crib. For added stability, drill pilot holes in crib top rail that rests against dresser unit. Drive three 2-inch by No. 6 flat-head screws through rail into dressers.

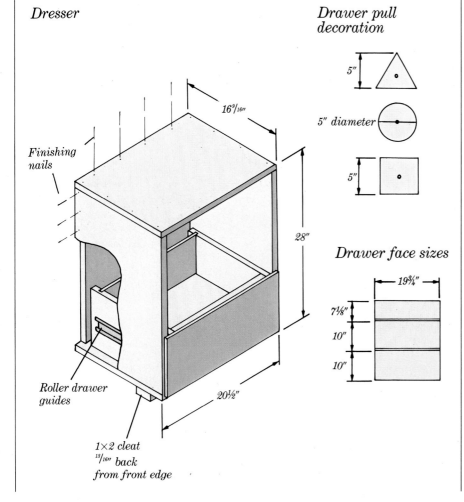

Dresser

Finishing nails

16⁹/₁₆"

28"

Roller drawer guides

20½"

1×2 cleat ¹³/₁₆" back from front edge

Drawer pull decoration

5"

5" diameter

5"

Drawer face sizes

19¾"

7⅛"

10"

10"

Active, physical play is one of the ways children learn how the world works. Having space allocated where a variety of objects and playthings are easily accessible encourages creativity and experimentation in a nonjudgmental atmosphere.

OFF AND RUNNING
Three to Six Years Old

Between the ages of three and six, children are becoming skilled at jumping, skipping, and climbing. They use their hands with precision and take command of crayons, buttons, and building blocks.

Through physical activity and action, children begin to learn how things work. In their play they act out the roles of heroes and villains to help them overcome their fears and to try out roles in the grown-up world.

Enterprise

Preschoolers enjoy initiating their own games, and they make play structures out of almost anything. They like to assemble thematic representations of farms, circuses, airports, houses, and forts. This kind of play-acting may involve the use of hundreds of little toy pieces and require a fair amount of table or floor space.

Because preschoolers are ready and willing to undertake positive, constructive activities on their own, it is a good time to begin training children to pick up their belongings when they are finished playing. To make the job easier, they need convenient, easy-to-reach storage units (scaled-down closets, shelves, drawers, for example). The storage unit on page 79 treats possessions with respect and gives children an opportunity to be physically active as well. Taking care of possessions is a fairly natural inclination if encouraged and reinforced.

Physical Activity

Preschoolers love to make big sweeping movements while drawing. A large chalkboard or marker board is well used at this stage of development. Consider the easel on page 77, which offers plenty of room for drawing at standing height and allows free arm and shoulder movement.

Young children love climbing, jumping, and running just for the joy of using their bodies. If there are tall dressers or bookcases in the room, bolt them to the wall. If a youngster can't resist the urge to climb to reach an object or play a game, the bolts will prevent accidental tipping. Keep a step stool handy to give children a longer reach without having to climb on the furniture.

Special Needs

Preschoolers graduate from the crib to some kind of a bed that is either low to the ground (a trundle bed or a mattress on the floor) or has a guardrail. When selecting the style, you might also want to consider how difficult it is to make the bed in the morning and change the sheets of a bunk or built-in bed. Mattress covers instead of sheet sets, and sleeping bags or loose comforters on top, may make the bed-making chore easy enough for your youngster.

Role-playing allows children to safely test out fantasies and explore the adult world. A mirror often becomes a welcome and cooperative playmate in the world of make believe.

STARRY NIGHTS CANOPY

Canopies add a touch of elegance to any bed, but more important for youngsters, they offer a bit of privacy. This quick and easy-to-build canopy turns a bed into a cozy retreat.

Canopies over beds are called testers, and the particular style shown here is known as a coat-hanger tester. Though usually supported by posts, this tester is hung by cords attached to the ceiling. Before you start construction, establish suitable anchor points for the cords—attach screw eyes directly into ceiling joists if you can. If the joist spacing is not right, attach two boards to ceiling and screw each into two or more joists. Attach screw eyes for the canopy into these boards. Hang the canopy from 4 points to avoid sway.

1. Cut 2 pieces of ³/₈-inch or ¹/₂-inch plywood 6 inches shorter than the length of mattress. Out of a wood closet pole, cut 3 pieces as long as the mattress is wide.

2. Transfer outline of your design onto the plywood and cut it out with a saber saw. Apply sanding sealer and sand edges and surfaces to be painted. Reapply sealer as necessary, then sand again. When smooth, prime the surface. Transfer entire design onto the surface and paint it.

3. Place panels back-to-back and drill ¹/₈-inch pilot holes at the points where the poles will traverse. Also drill ³/₃₂-inch pilot holes in ends of wood poles. Position panels and poles and fasten with 2-inch by No. 10 round-head screws and washers.

4. Drill ¹/₄-inch-diameter holes, ¹/₂-inch-deep into poles ¹/₄ inch from each end. Glue ¹/₄- by 1-inch dowels into these holes. (Dowels act as stops to keep rope from sliding toward the center of poles.) Tie ¹/₄-inch or ³/₈-inch rope around poles in a bowline knot, as shown.

With help, lift canopy and tie it with rope to the screw eyes. After making necessary adjustments to level the canopy, tie the rope off with a figure 8 knot. Check tightness of knots regularly.

5. Cut and hem a piece of fabric to serve as the drape. Sew weights into hems. Drape fabric over poles. To hold fabric in position and prevent sagging, glue Velcro fastening tape to the poles; sew a matching piece to the back of fabric where poles and fabric meet.

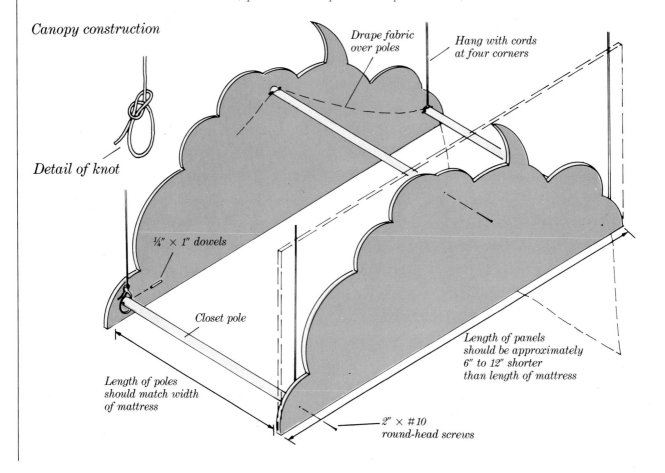

Canopy construction

Drape fabric over poles

Hang with cords at four corners

Detail of knot

¹/₄" × 1" dowels

Closet pole

Length of panels should be approximately 6" to 12" shorter than length of mattress

Length of poles should match width of mattress

2" × #10 round-head screws

Partially enclosing spaces with a canopy provides a little privacy and a feeling of security. The charming, easy-to-build design shown here incorporates a sun and stars motif. Use this motif or create one of your own.

Beautifully crafted of solid wood, this easel has many uses. Add casters to the hard-to-tip design and the easel becomes mobile.

EASEL

*T*he design of this easel allows height and size adjustments of the work surface. If you wish, add casters to make the easel mobile.

This easel will hold a chalkboard, marker board, stretched canvas, or roll paper, as well as art supplies.

Easel Frame Assembly

1. Out of straight 1 by 3s cut 2 main uprights 72 inches long. Chamfer corners on top end, then measure down 14 inches and drill a row of 26 centered holes $5/16$-inch in diameter at $1\frac{1}{2}$-inch intervals.

Drill a single $5/16$-inch hole $1\frac{1}{4}$ inches from bottom of each upright. Assemble pieces into a "ladder" by attaching two 1 by 4 crosspieces 21 inches long to back edges of uprights. Position one crosspiece 8 inches from top of uprights; the other 8 inches from bottom. Attach crosspieces with glue and $1\frac{1}{2}$-inch wallboard screws. Drill pilot holes with $3/8$-inch-diameter by $1/8$-inch-deep counterbores for screws.

2. From 1 by 4 stock cut 2 vertical footboards 28 inches long and 2 horizontal footboards $22\frac{1}{2}$ inches long for easel base. Drill a $5/16$-inch hole 12 inches from front end of each vertical foot board, centered across width of board. Cut a $1\frac{1}{2}$-inch, 45-degree chamfer on each upper corner. For gussets, cut four 3-inch right triangles from 1-by stock. Using glue and $1\frac{1}{2}$-inch wallboard screws, assemble base pieces as shown. Make sure that assembly is square.

3. Make adjustable back brace from 2 pieces of 1 by 3. Cut a piece 48 inches long for upper section and rout a $1/2$-inch slot 20 inches long starting 2 inches from bottom end (see illustration). Cut a 34-inch piece for lower section. Drill two $5/16$-inch holes 8 inches apart with first hole 2 inches from top of board.

Assemble brace by placing two $5/16$-inch carriage bolts through holes in lower section and through slot in upper section. Secure bolts with washers and wing nuts.

Attach $1\frac{1}{2}$-inch butt hinges to each end of brace assembly, as shown. Screw hinges to easel frame.

Paper Holder

1. Out of 1 by 3 stock, cut and drill end pieces as shown in illustration. From the same stock, cut a crosspiece 21 inches long, then rout a $1/2$-inch-wide by 16-inch-long slot through it. Attach end pieces to crosspiece using glue and $1\frac{1}{2}$-inch wallboard screws.

2. Cut dowel supports from 1-by stock and rout $1/2$-inch-wide by $3/8$-inch-deep grooves in them as shown. Using glue and screws, attach supports, positioning them $1\frac{1}{4}$-inches from ends of crosspiece assembly. Drill pilot holes with counterbores from back of crosspiece and use $1\frac{1}{4}$-inch by No. 6 flat-head screws. Measure distance between grooves in dowel supports and cut $1/2$-inch diameter dowel to fit.

3. Make retainers to hold chalkboard in place from 1 by 4 stock. Cut two 3-inch triangles, then cut each to trapezoid shape as shown. Drill a $1/2$-inch-diameter hole in back of each trapezoid for dowel. Glue and insert 2-inch lengths of $1/2$-inch-diameter dowel. Drill two $1/2$-inch holes through

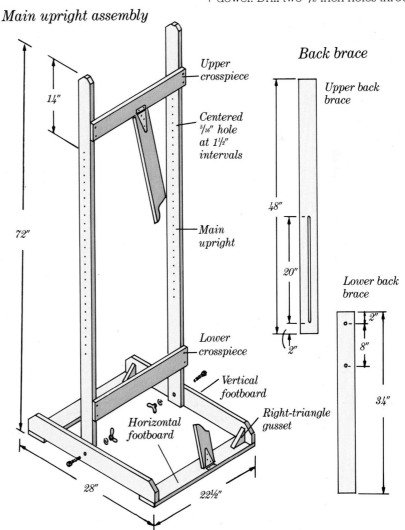

Main upright assembly

Upper crosspiece

Centered $5/16"$ hole at $1\frac{1}{2}"$ intervals

Main upright

Lower crosspiece

Vertical footboard

Horizontal footboard

Right-triangle gusset

14"

72"

28"

$22\frac{1}{2}"$

Back brace

Upper back brace

48"

20"

2"

Lower back brace

2"

8"

34"

¾-inch-diameter dowel, then cut dowel into two 1½-inch lengths.

After positioning retainer assemblies in crosspiece slot, push ¾-inch dowels on to ends of ½-inch dowels.
4. Use ⁵⁄₁₆-inch carriage bolts with wing nuts to attach paper holder assembly to main uprights of easel.

Tray

1. Cut 2 pieces of 1 by 4 to 21 inches. Glue and screw these together and attach end pieces using 1½-inch wallboard screws. Cut a 22½-inch length of 1-inch lattice

and glue it to front of tray.
2. Form top of tray by gluing on a 24-inch piece of ½-inch by 2-inch lattice. Cut a slot in lattice to allow paper from roll to be fed through. Glue a 21-inch piece of 1-inch lattice to front edge of tray top to keep chalkboard from sliding off.
3. Attach this assembly to main uprights with ⅜-inch carriage bolts and wing nuts.

Chalkboard

1. Out of ³⁄₁₆-inch hardboard cut a piece 22 inches by 34 inches. Paint with chalkboard paint.

2. From 1 by 2 stock, cut 2 pieces 24 inches long and 2 pieces 36 inches long and miter their ends. Cut a ³⁄₁₆-inch slot ⅝-inch deep on inner edge of each piece. Assemble frame and chalkboard pieces with glue; hold in place with picture frame clamps until glue has set.

Finishing

Plug and fill screw holes, sand easel, and coat with shellac or varnish. Adjust tray to desired height and set paper holder assembly according to height of chalkboard.

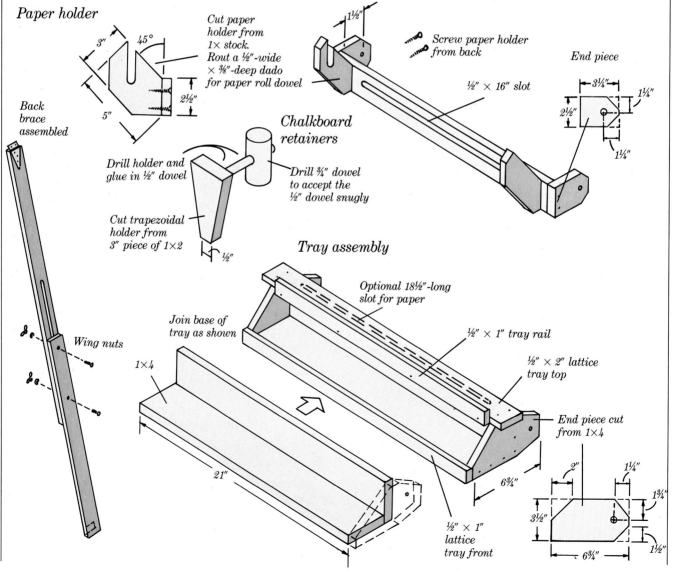

Paper holder

Cut paper holder from 1× stock. Rout a ½"-wide × ⅜"-deep dado for paper roll dowel

Screw paper holder from back

End piece

½" × 16" slot

Back brace assembled

Chalkboard retainers

Drill holder and glue in ½" dowel

Drill ¾" dowel to accept the ½" dowel snugly

Cut trapezoidal holder from 3" piece of 1×2

Tray assembly

Optional 18½"-long slot for paper

Join base of tray as shown

½" × 1" tray rail

½" × 2" lattice tray top

Wing nuts

1×4

End piece cut from 1×4

21"

6¾"

½" × 1" lattice tray front

3½"

6¾"

STORAGE CENTER

*The playful quality of this storage unit
makes it fun to put away belongings.
Once it is attached to the wall,
the unit becomes a climbing structure
for active play, too.*

I t's as fun to put things
away as it is to take
them out of this stor-
age center. Secret spaces
and crawl-through cubby-
holes make it a fantasy
play space as well.

Since this structure serves as both a
play and a storage center, attach it to
at least two wall studs for stability.

Main Structure

1. From 18-inch-wide strips of quality-grade ¾-inch plywood, cut 2 sides
58 inches long with 60-degree bevel
cuts at top, 2 shelves 46½ inches
long, and 2 shelves 24 inches long.
For side of closet, cut 1 piece 48
inches long by 18 inches wide. Saw a
14-inch-diameter hole in this piece.
Position hole so that its lower edge is
2 inches from end of board and it is
centered across width of board.
Round edges of hole and sand
smooth.
For closet roof, cut 2 pieces 18
inches wide by 12⅝ inches long with
parallel 60-degree bevel cuts on
ends. For main roof, cut 2 pieces 18
inches wide by 29 inches long with
parallel 60-degree bevel cuts.
2. Out of 1 by 2 stock, cut 2 ledger
boards 17¼ inches long for closet-
roof support. Nail one to left wall, one
to center wall flush at back edge.
3. Assemble pieces to form basic
structure as shown in illustration.
Glue and nail joints. To stabilize unit,
glue and nail 1 by 3 rails 48 inches
long to the front; attach one across
bottom front of structure and one
across top shelf. Note that upper rail
is flush with lower edge of top shelf.
4. Lay assembled unit on its back on
a sheet of ¼-inch plywood so that
sides and bottom of unit are flush with
edges of plywood. Trace roofline onto
plywood sheet. Cut plywood and

and glue and nail it to back of unit. Complete by adding small gable pieces cut from ¾-inch plywood on front of main roof and closet roof.

Ladder

1. Out of 1 by 3 stock cut 2 rails, each 57¾ inches long. Cut two 6-inch squares from ¾-inch plywood.

Attach plywood squares to outside top of each rail using glue and 1¼-inch by No. 6 flat-head screws as shown in illustration.

Starting 6 inches from bottom of rails, drill 1-inch holes to accept rungs. Holes should be centered and drilled every 6 inches.
2. Cut 8 rungs 14 inches long from 1-inch birch or oak dowel. Attach rungs to rails by applying glue to dowel holes and inserting dowels.

Help organize a room with this multipurpose storage unit constructed from a single sheet of quality-grade plywood. Add a ladder with rollers to slide from side to side, and children can reach every shelf.

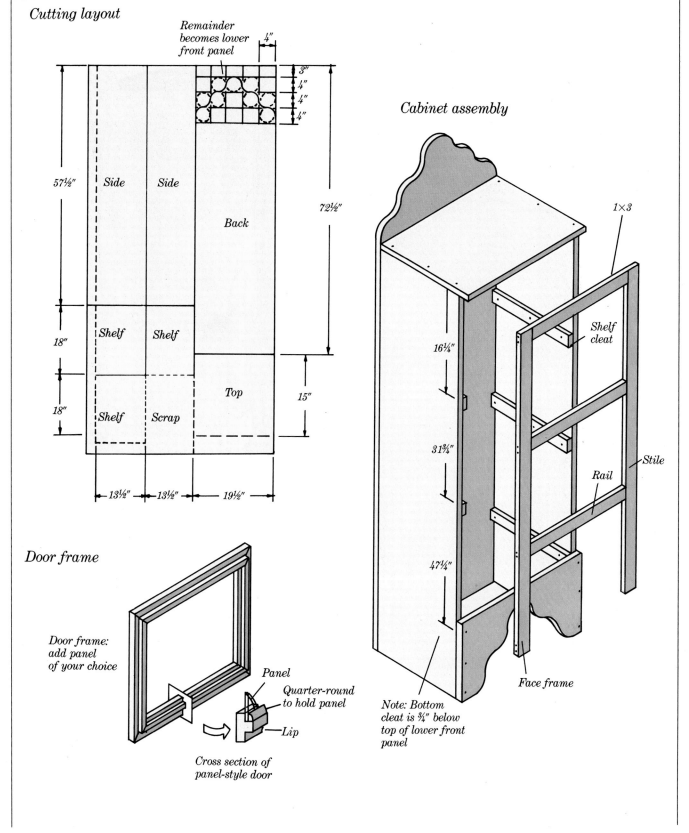

Cutting layout

Remainder becomes lower front panel

4"

3"
4"
4"
4"

57½"

Side   Side

Back

72½"

18"

Shelf   Shelf

18"

Shelf   Scrap

Top

15"

13½"   13½"   19½"

Cabinet assembly

1×3

Shelf cleat

16¼"

31¾"

Rail

Stile

47¼"

Face frame

Note: Bottom cleat is ¾" below top of lower front panel

Door frame

Door frame: add panel of your choice

Panel

Quarter-round to hold panel

Lip

Cross section of panel-style door

ADJUSTABLE STUDY DESK

*T*his study desk is made of only five pieces of plywood; some 2 by 4s; laminate, if desired; and hardware. The height of the work surface can be adjusted from 18 inches to 28 inches, which makes it suitable for six- to eleven-year-olds.

1. Out of ³/₄-inch plywood cut back panel 42¹/₂ inches by 42 inches; 2 side panels 20³/₄ inches by 33 inches; desk top 42¹/₂ inches by 20 inches; and shelf 42¹/₂ inches by 5 inches.
2. For a plastic laminate surface on desk top, cut a piece of laminate ¹/₂ inch larger than desk top. Coat desk top and back of laminate with contact cement. When cement is dry, bring two pieces together, taking care to have a ¹/₄-inch overhang at all edges. Use a roller to insure contact between laminate and top. Trim excess at edges with a router and laminate trimmer bit.

On underside of desk top, glue and clamp a 42¹/₂-inch kiln-dried 2 by 4, centered between front and back edges, and a 3¹/₂-inch-square block of 2 by 4, centered and flush with the back edge. These 2 by 4s help support the adjustable top.
3. Lay out and cut steps in top of back piece with a saber saw. The cuts are 8¹/₂ inches wide and stepped at 3-inch intervals. Also cut an 8¹/₂-inch by 3-inch step in upper front corner of each side piece.
4. Carefully rout a ¹/₄-inch-wide vertical slot in each side piece and in center of back piece. Start the ¹/₄-inch by 10-inch slots 17 inches from bottom of each piece. When making slots, clamp a guide board to each sheet to ensure a straight cut.
5. For height adjustment knobs, buy three 2-inch wooden knobs. Enlarge the hole in each to ³/₁₆-inch and epoxy a ¹/₄- by 3¹/₂-inch threaded stud into hole.
6. Glue side panels to back panel. Drill pilot holes, then drive wallboard screws spaced at 5-inch intervals to add stability. (Pilot holes are necessary because screws are close to edge of plywood.)

On sides mark position of shelf, 3 inches down from top of sides. Drill pilot holes and screw shelf to back and sides.
7. Drill ³/₁₆-inch diameter holes in ends of long 2 by 4 and in outer edge of 2 by 4 block glued to bottom of desk surface. Locate these pilot holes so they line up with slots in sides and back of desk.
8. Using router or abrasive paper, round off corners of desk. Sand entire unit, prime or seal, and coat with oil paint or varnish. Latex is not recommended for this project. Set aside until completely dry.
9. To set height of desk top, lay table on its back and place adjustable work surface in position. Screw threaded stud through side slot and into ³/₁₆-inch hole in 2 by 4. Repeat on opposite side. Set desk in upright position and install third knob assembly. Check height, adjust if necessary, and tighten knobs to secure top.

Promote good study habits with this adjustable study desk. Desk-top height adjusts to suit six-year-olds through teenagers. The desk shown was spray-painted and then stenciled.

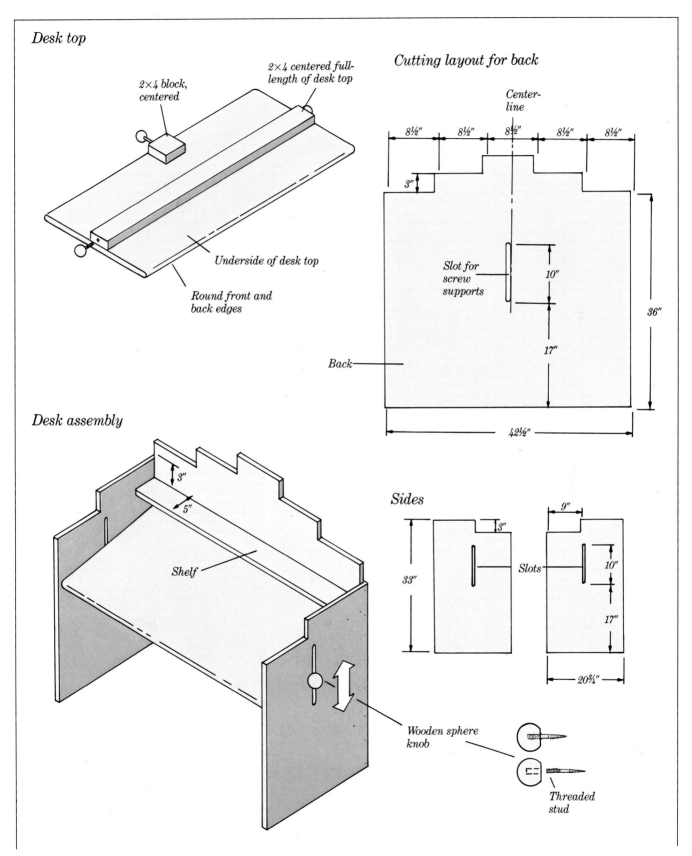

Desk top

2×4 block, centered

2×4 centered full-length of desk top

Underside of desk top

Round front and back edges

Cutting layout for back

Center-line

8½" 8½" 8½" 8½" 8½"

3"

Slot for screw supports

10"

36"

17"

Back

42½"

Desk assembly

3"

5"

Shelf

Sides

3"

9"

33"

Slots

10"

17"

20¾"

Wooden sphere knob

Threaded stud

COUNTRY TRUNDLE BED

Traditional furniture styles can be well suited to a child's sense of whimsy. The trundle space under the bed can be used as either a storage bin or a pull-out bed for overnight guests.

Since the trundle unit must be able to roll underneath the main bed, the height of the main structure is important. This design is based on a maximum lower mattress thickness of 7 inches and casters of an overall height of 2 inches. If you use a mattress thicker than 7 inches or casters taller than 2 inches, or plan to store bulky items in the bin, adjust the height of the legs on the upper bed accordingly.

Solid-core plywood is suggested for this project because cutouts and designs are easily cut with a saber saw, but feel free to select the wood of your choice. This is a good project for finer woods, if you have the skill.

Upper Bed

1. Out of 2 by 10s cut 2 side rails 84¼ inches long. Out of 2 by 2s cut 4 lengths 16 inches long to form tops of rails; rough shape one end of each. Glue and nail shaped 2 by 2s to top

With its richly colored stain and sturdy construction, this trundle bed evokes old-world charm, yet pleases even today's youngsters. Add detailing, such as the contrasting color finials and tree stencil, to personalize the bed.

of side rails (one at each end). When glue is dry, do final shaping and smoothing.

2. Cut 4 bedposts 34 inches long or to a height to accommodate objects in trundle unit. Cut dadoes to match actual dimensions of side rail assemblies. Bottom edge of dado should be 12¼ inches from floor level (higher if you require more space under bed).

3. Lay a pair of legs on a flat work surface dadoes up. (To prevent drilling into work surface, set legs on pieces of 2-inch scrap wood.) Place rail assembly into dadoes, line it up, then drill two ¼-inch-holes through rail and legs into scrap wood. Turn legs over and drill ¾-inch-diameter counterbores 1 inch deep. Repeat procedure to attach other pair of legs to second rail. Using ¼-inch by 3-inch carriage bolts, bolt legs and rails together. Place washers under nuts.

4. Cut headboard and footboard from ¾-inch solid-core plywood or the wood of your choice. Use three 2-inch by No. 8 flat-head wood screws to attach head- and footboards to insides of leg-rail assemblies. This forms basic bed frame.

5. Measure and cut 2 by 2s for cleats to support mattress base. Glue cleats to inside of rails, flush at the bottom. Drive a 2½-inch by No. 8 flat-head screw every 6 inches. Install cleats on inner face of head- and footboard at same height as side cleats.

6. Out of ½-inch plywood cut mattress base to fit within bed frame, or position 1 by 4 slats that span the side cleats to support mattress.

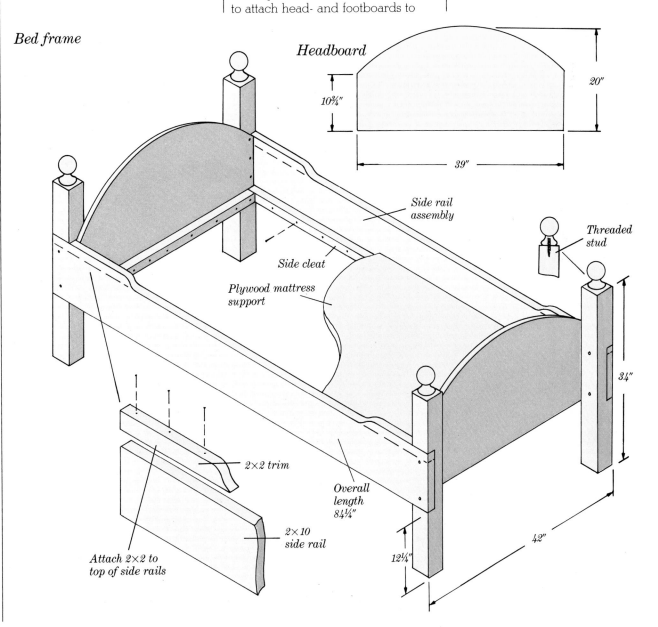

Bed frame

Headboard

10¾"

20"

39"

Side rail assembly

Threaded stud

Side cleat

Plywood mattress support

2×2 trim

34"

Attach 2×2 to top of side rails

2×10 side rail

Overall length 84¼"

12¼"

42"

7. Finish upper-bed assembly with decorative wood knobs on posts. Drill matching holes in posts and knobs and attach with double-ended lag studs. To cover counterbores in legs, insert ¾-inch wood cap plugs. (If bed might be disassembled in the future, don't glue plugs.)

Trundle Unit

1. Cut 4 side pieces out of ¾-inch plywood or 1 by 10 board stock. Cut 2 at 76½ inches; 2 at 39 inches. Lay out cutouts on the 2 long sides; cut with a saber saw.
2. Out of 2 by 2, cut 2 side cleats 75 inches long and 2 end cleats 36 inches long. Glue cleats to inside of side pieces, flush at bottom and inset equally from ends. Secure with 2¼-inch by No. 8 round-head screws.
3. Glue trundle frame together. Drill 4 pilot holes and countersinks at each corner, then drive 1¾-inch by No. 8 flat-head screws. Cut triangular braces to reinforce corners and glue them inside frame.
4. Measure and cut a piece of ½-inch plywood to support mattress, remembering to notch corners of wood to clear braces. Screw base to cleats with 4 screws along the sides and 3 along the ends (wallboard screws work well for this).
5. Flip box over and attach casters on the underside of the base.

Finishing

Fill, sand, stain, and seal the wood. As you sand, be sure to round off any sharp corners. This design is complemented by richly colored stain and a flat finish.

Trundle construction

Corner block glued in for added strength

2×2 cleats

2" casters

½" plywood mattress support

¾" plywood or 1×10 board

9¼"

76½"

40½"

Detail: Trundle under bed

1" space

7" mattress

¾" plywood

1½" ledger

12¼"

9¼"

2"

INDEX

Designers/Architects

Christopher Alexander
Berkeley, Calif.
Pages 8 (below), 12 (top)

Mary Applegarth
San Francisco, Calif.
Page 30

Claus Brigman
Novato, Calif.
Pages 6, 11 (left), 35 (top), 42 (top), 47,

Mary Edwards Collection
San Francisco, Calif.
Front cover, pages 10, 52, 58, 90
(rugs and table set)

Julie Salle Haas
San Francisco, Calif.
Pages 9, 35 (below), 36 (below), 85
(copyrighted stencil designs)

Linda Kilgore and Liddy Schmitt
San Francisco, Calif.
Page 35 (below)

Caryl Kurtzman, Designer, ADIA
Kenneth Kurtzman, Architect, AIA
Piedmont, Calif.
Pages 14, 41 (lower left), 84

Catherine LeBlanc Interiors,
represented by Decorator Previews
San Francisco, Calif.
Page 46 (top)

Anne Levine
Albany, Calif.
Pages 6, 13, 42 (top and below), 47

Toby S. Levy, AIA
San Francisco, Calif.
Pages 7, 72

Robert Mueller, AIA
Berkeley, Calif.
Page 40

Osburn Design
San Francisco, Calif.
Pages 34 (top, lower left), 41 (top,
lower right)

Marilyn Roy
Sassie Lassie Designs
Diablo, Calif.
Page 36 (top)

Antonio Torrice
Just Between Friends
San Francisco, Calif.
Page 20

Ron and Pam Unkefer
San Francisco, Calif.
Pages 8 (top), 11 (right), 32
(floor by The Painted Ladies
Kentfield, Calif.)

Special Thanks

Marion Fredman, Such A Business
John McCormick, MGI Studios
Michel Rabaste
Mary K. Loving
Mrs. Christensen
Martin Anderson, Principal,
Coventry Elementary School
LIMN Company
Katite Gimucio
Barbara Waldman, Decorator
Previews
Juvenile Lifestyles

U.S. Measure and Metric Measure Conversion Chart

	Formulas for Exact Measures				*Rounded Measures for Quick Reference*		
	Symbol	*When you know:*	*Multiply by*	*To find:*			
Mass (Weight)	oz	ounces	28.35	grams	1 oz		= 30 g
	lb	pounds	0.45	kilograms	4 oz		= 115 g
	g	grams	0.035	ounces	8 oz		= 225 g
	kg	kilograms	2.2	pounds	16 oz	= 1 lb	= 450 kg
					32 oz	= 2 lb	= 900 kg
					36 oz	= 2¼ lb	= 1000g (a kg)
Volume	tsp	teaspoons	5.0	milliliters	¼ tsp	= 1/24 oz	= 1 ml
	tbsp	tablespoons	15.0	milliliters	½ tsp	= 1/12 oz	= 2 ml
	fl oz	fluid ounces	29.57	milliliters	1 tsp	= ⅙ oz	= 5 ml
	c	cups	0.24	liters	1 tbsp	= ½ oz	= 15 ml
	pt	pints	0.47	liters	1 c	= 8 oz	= 250 ml
	qt	quarts	0.95	liters	2 c (1 pt)	= 16 oz	= 500 ml
	gal	gallons	3.785	liters	4 c (1 qt)	= 32 oz	= 1 liter
	ml	milliliters	0.034	fluid ounces	4 qt (1 gal)	= 128 oz	= 3¾ liter
Length	in.	inches	2.54	centimeters	⅜ in.	= 1 cm	
	ft	feet	30.48	centimeters	1 in.	= 2.5 cm	
	yd	yards	0.9144	meters	2 in.	= 5 cm	
	mi	miles	1.609	kilometers	2½ in.	= 6.5 cm	
	km	kilometers	0.621	miles	12 in. (1 ft)	= 30 cm	
	m	meters	1.094	yards	1 yd	= 90 cm	
	cm	centimeters	0.39	inches	100 ft	= 30 m	
					1 mi	= 1.6 km	
Temperature	°F	Fahrenheit	⁵⁄₉ (after subtracting 32)	Celsius	32°F	= 0°C	
					68°F	= 20°C	
	°C	Celsius	⁹⁄₅ (then add 32)	Fahrenheit	212°F	= 100°C	
Area	$in.^2$	square inches	6.452	square centimeters	1 $in.^2$	= 6.5 cm^2	
	ft^2	square feet	929.0	square centimeters	1 ft^2	= 930 cm^2	
	yd^2	square yards	8361.0	square centimeters	1 yd^2	= 8360 cm^2	
	a.	acres	0.4047	hectares	1 a.	= 4050 m^2	